Tropic Of Genius

Exploring The World Of Henry Miller

GEW Humanities Group

Global East-West. London

Copyright © 2025 by GEW Humanities
World Literature.
A Global East-West Series.
All rights reserved. No part of this book may be reproduced in any manner without written permission, except in the case of brief quotations incorporated in critical articles and reviews.
First printing, 2025.

Contents

1. Preface by Hichem Karoui — 1
   A Literary Iconoclast

2. Origins — 14
   From Brooklyn to Bohemia

3. Tropic of Cancer — 27
   Breaking down boundaries

4. Parisian Muse — 40
   The City of Liberation

5. The Art of Chaos — 53
   Crafting Tropic of Capricorn

6. The Rosy Crucifixion — 66
   Myth, Memory, and Madness

7. Exploring Philosophies — 79
   Miller's Intellectual Foundations

8. The Colossus of Maroussi — 92
   A Journey to Transcendence

9. Beyond Scandal: — 105
   Censorship and Literary Freedom

10.	Influences and Inspirations Nietzsche to Surrealism	118
11.	Literary Legacy Impact and Influence on the Beat Generation	132
12.	Letters and Essays Insight into the Human Condition	145
13.	Friends and Foes Anaïs Nin and Literary Circles	158
14.	A Philosopher of Everyday Life	170
15.	Controversy and Criticism Reception Through the Decades	184
16.	The Personal Odyssey A Search for Authenticity	199
17.	Conclusion Embracing Chaos, Celebrating Existence	209
Selective Bibliography		223

Preface by Hichem Karoui

A Literary Iconoclast

Setting the scene: historical context

At the beginning of the twentieth century, as Henry Miller began his literary career, the world was undergoing profound transformations. The aftermath of the First World War resounded with disillusionment and fervent societal reappraisal, leading to an era characterised by cultural upheaval and a fervent quest for new artistic expression. In the United States, the Roaring Twenties gave rise to a climate of liberation and experimentation, marked by the proliferation of jazz, the rise of women's rights and the flourishing of the Harlem Renaissance. At the same time, Europe was facing the consequences of war, witnessing the dissolution of empires and the birth of new ideologies.

Navigating this tumultuous context, Miller was immersed in the rebellious spirit of the times, when established norms were challenged and boundaries pushed back. The nascent modernist movement, with its rejection of traditional literary forms and its embrace of subjective experience, provided fertile ground for Miller's iconoclastic tendencies. Paris, in particular, emerged as a beacon for artists and writers seeking to escape the constraints of conservative societies. It was in this milieu that Miller found inspiration and solidarity in bohemian circles, which shared his contempt for conventional morality and artistic conventions.

At the same time, the political landscape of the inter-war period witnessed the consolidation of totalitarian regimes and the shadow of economic collapse. Fascism and communism vied for control, while the world teetered on the brink of a new global conflict. Against this backdrop, Miller's work represents an unequivocal challenge to social orthodoxy and an unwavering commitment to unfettered personal expression.

To understand Miller's literary impact, it is necessary to appreciate the seismic shifts underway: the clash between tradition and modernity, the emergence of psychoanalysis, the questioning of authority and the palpable tension that precedes cataclysmic events. It is in the crucible of this historical context that the figure of Henry Miller, with his fearless questioning of social mores and his relentless quest for authenticity, takes on its full importance.

Definition of iconoclasm in literature

Iconoclasm in literature embodies the daring act of questioning established norms and conventions in the field of artistic expression. It involves a deliberate departure from traditional paradigms, subverting societal expectations and defying conventional literary norms. The iconoclastic writer thus embodies literary rebellion and radical innovation, seeking to dismantle preconceived notions and provoke a reappraisal of entrenched ideologies. Basically, iconoclasm supports the ethic of disruption, deconstruction and reconstruction, aimed at redefining the limits of creativity and artistic discourse.

Iconoclasm in literature transcends mere non-conformity; it represents a bold attempt to confront orthodoxies, to undo orthodox narratives and to challenge the status quo. Iconoclastic literature dares to interrogate the essence of human experience, tackle taboo subjects and explore uncharted territory, harnessing the power of words to incite reflection, dissent and transformation. Through evocative prose and thought-provoking narratives, iconoclastic writers draw their readers into the vortex of new perspectives and wild intellectual landscapes, forcing them to confront the discomfort of uncertainty and the exhilaration of existential questioning.

Furthermore, iconoclasm in literature encourages a reconfiguration of language, style and narrative techniques, avoiding complacency and embracing the avant-garde. It transcends the mere subversion of norms; it is an ideological revolution woven into the fabric of every sentence, paragraph and chapter, engendering a palpable sense of ideological dissonance in the literary firmament. This act of creative insurrection imbues the narrative with a sense of urgency, infuses it with a certain nervousness and imbues it with the raw authenticity that resonates with unyielding truth. The iconoclastic writer thus becomes the harbinger of change, urging readers to abandon the safe harbours of familiarity and embark on transformative odysseys of inquiry and introspection.

For the iconoclastic writer, literary boundaries are not to be respected, but rather dismantled, transcended and reinvented. This unwavering commitment to artistic disruption animates the pages with an unrivalled dynamism, injecting vitality into the ossified canons of tradition. Every word becomes a harbinger of rebellion, every page a battleground for ideological upheaval, and every story an epiphany of emancipation. In essence, iconoclasm in literature heralds the arrival of a new age of literary consciousness, ushering in an era in which the art of storytelling becomes an act of defiance, and the written word emerges as a powerful instrument of societal metamorphosis and cultural revolution.

The birth of a maverick writer

Born into the vibrant cultural milieu of early twentieth-century Brooklyn, Henry Miller's formative years were marked by an unquenchable thirst for knowledge and a rebellious spirit that set him apart from his peers. The convergence of Brooklyn's diverse immigrant communities, artistic enclaves and intellectual ferment provided fertile ground for the young Miller's burgeoning curiosity and relentless pursuit of artistic expression.

The influence of his tumultuous upbringing, combined with exposure to the kaleidoscope of human experience, laid the groundwork for Miller's eventual emergence as a literary iconoclast. Deeply influenced by the eclectic mix of cultures, languages and ideas that surrounded him, Miller developed an acute sensitivity to the human condition and an insatiable appetite for understanding the complex interplay of emotions and desires that define our existence.

However, it was not only external influences that shaped Miller's worldview; his introspective nature led him to delve deeply into the realms of literature, philosophy and art. His early encounters with provocative works of literature, groundbreaking philosophical treatises and avant-garde artistic expressions served as catalysts for the formation of his distinct artistic voice, one that challenged convention and questioned societal norms.

Navigating the labyrinthine streets of Brooklyn, Miller encountered transformative figures who left an indelible imprint on her evolving sensibility. From impassioned discussions with bohemian poets to impassive exchanges with enigmatic philosophers, each interaction contributed to the tapestry of his intellectual development, propelling him to embrace the role of maverick writer.

In this crucible of self-discovery, Miller forged an intrinsic link between his inner turmoil and outer chaos, harnessing the raw energy of his experiences to fuel his creative endeavours. His unquenchable thirst for authentic expression propelled him on a trajectory that transcended the traditional boundaries of literature, paving the way for uncharted narrative territory that would challenge readers and critics alike.

The spark of rebellion and creativity that ignited in Miller during his formative years in Brooklyn continued to glow, propelling him into the uncharted landscape of literary innovation and challenge. It ultimately consolidated his status as a maverick writer who dared to defy the constraints of conventional narrative and narrative structure.

Early influences and artistic foundations

Henry Miller's formative years were enriched by a wide range of influences that would shape his distinctive literary style. Born in 1891 in the vibrant cultural landscape of Brooklyn, New York, Miller was raised in a household that valued artistic expression and intellectual discourse. The ethics of the early twentieth century, with its tumultuous social and political upheavals, had a profound effect on the young Miller, instilling in him a sense of rebellion and a desire for unconventional self-expression.

During his formative years, Miller found inspiration in the works of influential writers such as Walt Whitman, D.H. Lawrence and Knut Hamsun, whose raw and provocative stories challenged the norms and conventions of society. In addition to literary influences, Miller was drawn to the avant-garde art movements of the time, particularly the radical experimentation of the Dadaists and Surrealists. The convergence of these diverse influences instilled in Miller a fervent belief in the unrestricted exploration of human experience through art.

In the context of nascent modernism, Miller embarked on a journey of self-discovery and artistic exploration, ultimately seeking to free himself from the constraints of traditional narrative forms and moral conventions. His voracious appetite for literature, philosophy and the arts propelled him on a fervent quest for authenticity and unfettered creativity. In addition, his bohemian lifestyle and unwavering curiosity led him to immerse himself in the rich cultural milieu of Greenwich Village, where he met kindred spirits and immersed himself in a multitude of perspectives that would later inform his writing.

These early experiences coincided to form the bedrock of Miller's artistic foundations, laying the groundwork for the rebellious spirit and uncompromising ethos that would define his literary work. Through a close examination of these formative influences and artistic foundations, we can begin to unravel the intricacies of Miller's remarkable evolution from aspiring writer to powerful literary iconoclast.

A divergent path: The decision to break up

As we move further along the tumultuous path of the literary iconoclast, it becomes clear that a critical moment occurred when the aspiring writer was faced with a crucial decision: to break away from the conventions of the established literary canon and chart an idiosyncratic course. This divergence from the well-trodden paths of traditional storytelling embodies a bold leap of faith, underpinned by a resolute determination to defy societal norms and push the boundaries of artistic expression.

The decision to break with the normative constructs of literature stemmed from a deep dissatisfaction with the dominant modes of creative discourse. It reflected an innate desire for unbridled authenticity and an unshakeable commitment to unfettered personal expression. This bold stance heralded a paradigm shift in the author's artistic ethos, provoking a seismic break with the homogeneity of dominant literary paradigms.

In elucidating this crucial transitional phase, we discern the interplay of various influences and philosophical principles that galvanised the author's bold venture into uncharted literary terrain. The intellectual effervescence that reigned in the writer's milieu served as a crucible for forging radical ideologies and avant-garde sensibilities, a concoction that would feed the tapestry of their rebellious literary odyssey.

Moreover, taking a divergent direction testifies to an unyielding desire to challenge the ossified rules of conventional storytelling and chart a new narrative course. It was motivated by an unshakeable belief in the redemptive power of unorthodox literary innovation, enshrining the quest for unadulterated artistic freedom at the heart of the project.

The stratagem of breaking with preconceived literary mores testifies not only to the writer's indomitable spirit, but also to his unwavering commitment to deconstructing and reconstructing the very scaffolding of narrative. This marked departure has unveiled a fertile landscape for innovative narratives that reflect the complexities of human existence in an unabashedly authentic way.

As we explore this profound metamorphosis in the author's creative evolution, we are forced to confront the profound implications of the societal upheaval and cultural revolt that underpinned this divergence. Indeed, the decision to break away resonates as a milestone in the author's personal journey, but also as a testament to the ongoing evolution of art and literature themselves.

The philosophies that shaped the iconoclast

Henry Miller's literary rebellion was informed by a dynamic and multifaceted set of philosophies that formed the basis of his unique narrative. At the heart of Miller's approach is his deep commitment to existentialist thought, a philosophy that emphasises individual experience, freedom and the search for meaning in a seemingly chaotic world. Embracing the principles of existentialism, Miller rejects traditional norms and societal expectations, choosing instead to delve into the raw, unfiltered essence of human existence.

In addition, philosophical concepts such as nihilism and the absurd permeate Miller's work, echoing the disillusionment and disorientation experienced by individuals in the aftermath of the First World War. Through his writing, Miller confronted the absurdity of life and its inherent lack of meaning, presenting an austere yet profound interpretation of the human condition. His exploration of nihilistic themes reflects his desire to challenge established conventions and provoke introspection.

In addition to existentialism and nihilism, Miller's work also reflects influences from Eastern philosophies such as Zen Buddhism and Taoism. He sought to capture the fluidity and impermanence of existence, drawing inspiration from the interconnectedness of all things and the concept of embracing the present moment. This infusion of Eastern thought enriched Miller's stories with a sense of transcendence and spiritual awareness, underlining his quest for inner liberation and self-realisation.

Miller's engagement with psychoanalytic theories, particularly those of Sigmund Freud and Carl Jung, also shaped his approach to character development and narrative structure. Delving into the depths of the human psyche, Miller illuminated the complexities of desire, repression and the unconscious, interweaving his psychological knowledge with his bold, uninhibited prose.

The fusion of these different philosophies wove the tapestry of Miller's literary identity, making him an iconoclastic figure who defied convention and fearlessly navigated the uncharted terrain of human consciousness. By wielding the power of ideas and philosophical inquiry, Miller harnessed a potent force that compelled readers to confront their assumptions, question their reality and embark on the transformative journey of self-discovery.

An unconventional approach to storytelling

Henry Miller's unconventional approach to storytelling challenged conventional norms of story structure and content. By adopting the stream-of-consciousness style, he ventured into uncharted literary territory, abandoning traditional linear plots and adopting a more organic and fluid form of expression. By avoiding the constraints of traditional narrative, Miller presented his readers with an immersive and raw depiction of human experience, delving into the depths of the human psyche with undisguised candour.

Rather than following a strictly chronological or logical sequence, Miller's stories often meander through memory, reflection and introspection. This non-linear approach allows her to capture the essence of lived experiences in a visceral and authentic way. Through this unconventional narrative, Miller has sought to dismantle the artificial boundaries between fiction and reality, inviting her audience to take part in a literary journey that reflects the unpredictable nature of existence itself.

Incorporating elements of autobiography and fiction, Miller has blurred the lines between the personal and the imaginary, weaving a tapestry of emotions, observations and philosophies. His protagonists often echo facets of his own personality, blurring the distinction between author and character. This blurring of boundaries gives his stories a sense of immediacy and truth, transcending the boundaries of traditional narrative to offer a deeper, more resonant exploration of the human condition.

Moreover, Miller's unorthodox approach goes beyond the thematic and structural aspects of his stories. He has fearlessly tackled taboo subjects such as sexuality, spirituality and existential contemplation with unflinching honesty and fervour. By embracing these controversial themes, Miller has challenged societal norms and provoked powerful reactions from his readers, sparking intense debate and discussion. This bold and intrepid approach to storytelling made Miller a trailblazer, pushing the boundaries of literature and paving the way for future generations of writers to explore complex and provocative subjects.

Ultimately, Henry Miller's unconventional storytelling not only transformed the literary landscape, but also left an indelible mark on the collective consciousness of his audience. Through his bold and unorthodox narrative approach, Miller was able to capture the nuances of human experience with unparalleled depth and authenticity, forever cementing his legacy as a literary iconoclast.

A controversial voice

In the literary landscape of the early twentieth century, Henry Miller emerged as a controversial and polarising figure, whose voice challenged traditional norms and conventions. His approach to taboo subjects, his unrestrained exploration of human desires and his often explicit depiction of sexuality became the hallmark of his work, positioning him as a provocative and controversial figure in the world of literature. Miller's willingness to venture into the raw, unfiltered aspects of human experience has distinguished him as a writer unafraid to confront the uncomfortable realities of life. This fearless approach to storytelling has offended society's taboos and made Miller an iconoclast, attracting both ardent admirers and vehement detractors. The visceral nature of his prose challenged readers to confront their own inhibitions and prejudices, inviting them to engage with the very essence of humanity. As a result, Miller's writings sparked fervent debates about censorship, artistic freedom and the limits of acceptable expression. This has led to a profound reassessment of the role of literature in shaping cultural values and challenging prevailing moral norms.

Despite the controversy surrounding his work, Miller's authentic depiction of the complexities of life resonated with those who sought unadorned truths and authentic human experiences in literature. His writing counterbalanced the prevailing sentimentality of the time, offering a frank and uncompromising exploration of the human condition. The shock value associated with Miller's stories often overshadowed the depth of his social commentary and philosophical insights, so his impact on literary discourse was both underestimated and fiercely contested. Miller's bold prose shook up the status quo, forcing readers to confront uncomfortable truths and prompting them to re-examine deeply entrenched societal norms. By introducing a controversial voice that challenged convention and shattered complacency, Miller's influence extended far beyond the realm of literature, challenging readers to question their assumptions and embrace the complexities inherent in human existence.

Reception: critical acclaim and reaction

Henry Miller's literary works have always provoked a provocative mix of critical acclaim and vehement reaction. The enfant terrible of American literature in his day, Miller left an indelible mark on the literary landscape with his penchant for the uncompromising revelation of human experience. On the one hand, his raw, no-holds-barred prose resonated deeply with a segment of readers eager for an authentic, unvarnished exploration of the complexities of life. Critics have praised her ability to peel back the veneers of society and expose the raw nerves of existence, hailing her fearlessness when it comes to tackling taboo subjects. His counter-cultural spirit, inherent in much of his writing, also resonated with those who sought to rebel against the constraints of convention and embrace a deeper understanding of the human condition. At the same time, Miller's disregard for societal norms and his willingness to tackle hitherto unexplored themes provoked fierce opposition from moral authorities and literary traditionalists.

His explicit depictions of sexuality, unconventional narrative structures and raw depictions of visceral themes frequently provoked accusations of obscenity and cultural decadence, leading to widespread censorship and alienation from established literary circles. The dichotomy between accolades and censures has shaped the reception of Miller's work, contributing to the ongoing debate about the merits and demerits of confronting society's taboos through art. Over the years, this controversial discourse has fuelled a sustained fascination with Miller's work, ensuring that his legacy remains as polarising as it is enduring. The evolution of critical perspectives on Miller's texts testifies to their profound impact and the enduring relevance of their provocative and iconoclastic character.

A legacy of innovation and rebellion

Henry Miller's uncompromising and revolutionary approach to literature has left an indelible mark on the literary landscape, ensuring his enduring legacy as a maverick and disrupter. His legacy of innovation and rebellion embodied in his work continues to resonate with readers and writers alike, transcending temporal and cultural boundaries, and inspiring generations to challenge the status quo. At the heart of this legacy is Miller's fearless exploration of the human experience, free from the constraints of societal norms or conventional storytelling paradigms.

Miller's bold prose, characterised by raw honesty and unflinching description of the human condition, has served as both a catalyst for introspection and a call to arms for those disillusioned by the veneer of polite society. His unvarnished depiction of life's underbelly, with its flaws, uncertainties and complexities, fundamentally altered the trajectory of autobiographical writing, laying bare emotional and psychological truths often deemed unavowable or taboo.

Moreover, Miller's rejection of traditional narrative structures and linear storytelling freed writers from the constraints of sequential chronology, encouraging them to adopt more intuitive and fragmentary forms of expression. His emphasis on subjectivity, spontaneity and stream-of-consciousness writing techniques revolutionised the art of literary composition, fostering a new wave of experimental fiction that moved away from rigid conventionality and embraced the chaos and discord of existence.

Beyond his innovative literary methods, Miller's rebellious spirit and unwavering commitment to personal freedom resonate as a testament to the power of the individual in the face of oppressive forces. By fearlessly challenging moral, social and artistic conventions, Miller asserted the autonomy of the artist and encouraged others to defy censorship, break taboos and confront the uncomfortable realities of their lived experiences.

In tracing Miller's legacy, it is impossible to ignore the profound impact he had on subsequent generations of writers, particularly the Beat Generation, whose counter-cultural ethos and rejection of materialism reflected Miller's own disillusionment with modernity. Kerouac, Ginsberg and Burroughs, among others, found kindred spirits in Miller's uninhibited prose, shaping a literary movement that sought to dismantle the veneer of societal hypocrisy and reclaim the authenticity of the individual voice.

Ultimately, Henry Miller's legacy lives on not only through his literary contributions, but also through the profound ideological and philosophical implications of his work. His unwavering commitment to artistic integrity, his defiance of societal constraints and his wholehearted embrace of the human experience continue to provoke contemplation, spark debate and inspire rebellious fervour in the pursuit of unbridled creativity and unfettered truth.

2

Origins
From Brooklyn to Bohemia

Modest beginnings: the backdrop of Brooklyn

Henry Miller's formative years in Brooklyn laid the foundations for the literary iconoclast he would become. Born on 26 December 1891 in the heart of Williamsburg, a neighbourhood teeming with cultural diversity and a working-class population, Miller was immersed in an environment that would leave an indelible mark on his art. The son of German immigrants, Miller experienced first-hand the struggles and triumphs of immigrant life, which undoubtedly fuelled his later exploration of existential themes and societal dissonance. The bustling streets and vibrant local characters of Brooklyn provided the young Miller with a colourful tapestry, rich in human experience and emotion, from which to write. The city's raw energy, culture clash and daily struggle for survival provided the backdrop for Miller's early perceptions of the world.

Family roots and early influences

Henry Miller's family roots and early influences provide a compelling backdrop to his unconventional literary journey. Born into a working-class family in Brooklyn in the late nineteenth century, Miller was surrounded by the sights, sounds and struggles of urban life. His parents' immigrant background and their struggle to make a living in a changing world left an indelible mark on the young Miller. The diversity of cultures and languages in his neighbourhood piqued his curiosity about the human experience and laid the foundations for his future writing explorations. Influenced by his family's stories of hardship, perseverance and resilience, Miller developed a keen awareness of the human condition from an early age. This early exposure to the complexities of life profoundly shaped his worldview and creative expression. In addition, his family's rich oral tradition instilled in him a deep appreciation of storytelling and language, igniting a passion that drove him to pursue his literary pursuits. His family's struggles with societal expectations and financial instability gave Miller a rebellious spirit, positioning him as a maverick against the norms of his time.

This environment, imbued with both struggle and vitality, laid the foundation for Miller's unique perspective on art, society and existence. As he matured, these formative influences became interwoven with his evolving artistic vision, defining the very essence of his work. Understanding the complex web of family ties and early environmental stimuli is therefore essential to unlocking the enigma of Henry Miller's literary legacy.

Early literary encounters: the first whispers of genius

During his adolescence, Henry Miller was drawn to the world of literature with an intense fervour. He voraciously devoured the works of famous authors and poets, finding solace and inspiration in the pages of their writings. Growing up in Brooklyn, a hotbed of cultural diversity and creative energy, the young Miller was exposed to a multitude of literary traditions and artistic movements, which would later serve as the basis for his own revolutionary contributions. It was during this formative period that Miller's uncanny ability to perceive profound beauty in the banal and monumental began to emerge. His keen sense of observation and insatiable curiosity set him on the path to introspection and enlightenment.

As he delved deeper into the world of words, themes of existentialism, spirituality and the human condition captured his imagination and shaped his nascent literary voice. His early encounters with the works of Whitman, Emerson and Thoreau instilled in him a deep appreciation of nature and its intrinsic link to the human experience, a theme that would later intertwine in his work.

Miller's voracious appetite for literature led him to spend countless nights immersed in the writings of Dostoyevsky, Tolstoy and Nietzsche, whose provocative philosophies influenced the evolution of his worldview. These seminal encounters lit a fire within Miller, igniting the flames of his own artistic expression and sowing the fertile ground from which his unique literary vision would blossom. As he grappled with the complexities of life, his burgeoning passion for narrative and the unyielding pursuit of truth manifested itself in the compositions etched into his journals. These early literary encounters would forever shape the trajectory of Miller's life, infusing his nascent creativity with a depth of understanding that transcended conventional narrative. Thus, the whispers of genius that echoed in the corridors of his mind during those formative years paved the way for the revolutionary prose that would define his legacy.

Adolescence and the desire to escape

Henry Miller's formative years were marked by an intense desire to escape the confines of a conventional existence. Having grown up in the industrial landscape of Brooklyn, he yearned for something extraordinary, something that transcended the mundane routines of everyday life. This restlessness is compounded by a growing awareness of the limits and constraints imposed by societal norms, forcing him to seek a path less travelled. In adolescence, Miller's thirst for exploration and adventure intensified, driving him towards a fervent desire for liberation. The torments of youth bred a rebellious spirit, captivated by the lure of unbridled freedom and uncharted territory. This insatiable thirst for novelty and defiance of conformity became the driving force behind his burgeoning aspirations.

Looking back, it is clear that this period of desire paved the way for the unconventional odyssey that would characterise Miller's adult life and literary endeavours. The palpable tension between the desire to escape and the gravitational pull of society's expectations set the stage for the tumultuous journey that awaited the young visionary. Amidst the smoke and clamour of Brooklyn, an irrepressible need to break free from convention took root in Miller's soul, pushing him inexorably towards unexplored horizons. It was during these formative years that the spirit of rebellion and the search for wild authenticity began to intertwine, shaping the contours of the enigmatic character who would later emerge. In retrospect, the fires of discontent raging in the adolescent Miller's heart would serve as a crucible for forging an indomitable spirit that would eventually defy the constraints of time and tradition, venturing into hitherto unexplored realms.

Academic tenacity: education and rebellion

Henry Miller's academic career was marked by a relentless tenacity and an irrepressible spirit of rebellion. Despite the many challenges he faced, Miller demonstrated an insatiable thirst for knowledge and defied the traditional constraints of education. His unwavering determination to forge his own path in academia was evident from an early age. Adopting a curriculum that went well beyond the bounds of conventional pedagogy, Miller avidly devoured literature, philosophy and the arts, seeking intellectual nourishment outside the confines of structured schooling.

His rebellious nature often clashed with the rigidity of institutional frameworks, leading him to frequently clash with authority figures. Yet this defiance fuelled his intellectual pursuits, prompting him to explore unconventional ideas and question established paradigms. Miller's education was not confined to the walls of the classroom; rather, it was cultivated through his voracious reading, passionate debates with like-minded intellectuals, and fervent engagement with the cultural zeitgeist of his time.

Although formal education provided a foundation, Miller's real learning came through independent exploration and critical enquiry. He avoided complacency, continually questioned societal norms and rejected intellectual dogma. This ethic of rebellion against entrenched ideologies laid the foundations for his later literary iconoclasm, as he sought to shatter literary conventions and redefine the boundaries of art and expression.

In the tumultuous context of societal upheaval, Miller's academic tenacity was tested as he faced the disillusionment of world events. The inter-war period, marked by economic turmoil and existential angst, profoundly shaped his worldview, infusing his studies with a sense of urgency and purpose. This turbulent environment gave rise to a fervent desire to discover the underlying truths of human existence, which led him to delve into the fields of philosophy, psychology and existentialism.

Throughout his intellectual odyssey, Miller's unwavering commitment to educational exploration has taken him beyond the boundaries of traditional scholarship, opening the door to innovative ideas and profound introspection. Through his unorthodox approach to learning, Miller transformed academic rebellion into a channel for intellectual liberation, laying the foundation for his transformative evolution as a writer and thinker.

The great American experience: formative journeys

Henry Miller's formative travels across America not only shaped his worldview, but also left an indelible mark on his nascent literary sensibility. From the bustling streets of New York to the idyllic landscapes of rural America, Miller embarked on a journey of self-discovery that profoundly influenced his later work. His encounters with diverse cultures, landscapes and people provided him with a rich tapestry of experiences that would find expression in his writing. As he travelled the country, he soaked up the vitality and dynamism of urban life, while finding solace and inspiration in the simplicity of rural existence. These contrasting experiences were the source of his creative energy, fostering a deep understanding of the many facets of American society.

Perhaps most importantly, these travels imbued Miller with a deep appreciation of the human condition, igniting his passion to capture its essence in his writing. His observations of social struggles, economic disparities and the complex interplay of human relationships became the foundation of his literary explorations. The Great Depression, which he witnessed first-hand, gave him a stark image of human resilience in the face of adversity, further shaping his empathetic approach to storytelling. Miller's sojourn across America was not just a physical journey; it was a spiritual odyssey that laid bare the complex connections between individuals and their environment. His encounters with the marginalized and the disenfranchised gave rise to a fervent desire to give a voice to the voiceless, to illuminate the often neglected facets of American life. With evocative prose and a keen sense of observation, Miller sought to convey the intrinsic dignity and tenacity of the American spirit, a theme that runs throughout his work. Ultimately, his travels across America helped him cultivate a nuanced and empathetic perspective that would come to define his literary legacy, marking the beginning of a lifelong quest to illuminate universal truths hidden in the fabric of everyday existence.

Love and loss: personal relationships that shape perspective

Henry Miller's early experiences of love and loss played a key role in shaping his unique perspective on life, love and the human condition. His relationships at this time were marked by both passion and turmoil, providing fertile ground for his later literary explorations. During his formative years, Miller was confronted with the complexities of intimate relationships, the tension between the desire for emotional fulfilment and the harsh realities of romantic entanglement. These experiences left an indelible mark on his creative psyche, infusing his work with raw emotional depth and introspective resonance. Reflecting on these tumultuous affairs, Miller delved into the depths of the human heart, exploring themes of desire, longing and the bittersweet nature of love. As he navigated the twists and turns of romantic relationships, he discovered profound insights into the vulnerabilities and complexities of human bonds, which would later manifest themselves in his evocative prose.

In the midst of the ebb and flow of love and loss, Miller discovered the transformative power of pain, which helped shape his worldview and artistic expression. In the crucible of emotional upheaval, he honed his ability to articulate the nuances of human emotion, creating stories that resonate with universal truth. These personal trials became the crucible of Miller's literary alchemy, catalysing his evolution from a simple observer of life to an astute interpreter of human experience. Through the prism of love and loss, Miller probed the essence of existence, capturing the fragility and resilience of the human spirit in his poignant descriptions of intimacy and separation. Every heartbreak and tender moment contributed to the tapestry of her narrative landscape, enriching her tale with a poignant authenticity that continues to captivate readers. Ultimately, Miller's exploration of love and loss laid the foundation for her work, imbuing her writing with an enduring emotional authenticity and timeless relevance.

Early struggles: From financial hardship to liberation

Henry Miller's early years were marked by major financial difficulties, which shaped his vision of the world and his approach to life. Born in the midst of economic turmoil, Miller was no stranger to hardship. His family was constantly confronted with financial instability, which engendered a sense of unease and precariousness that permeated his formative years. The burden of financial constraints weighed heavily on Miller, instilling in him a resilience and resourcefulness that were deeply ingrained in him.

Despite adversity, these challenges drove Miller to seek freedom from the constraints of poverty. His experiences taught him the value of perseverance and self-reliance, and instilled in him an unshakeable determination to chart his own course. This period of financial instability was the crucible in which Miller's determination was consolidated, laying the foundations for his later literary exploration of human struggle and resilience.

In facing financial hardship, Miller also became aware of the profound impact of socio-economic disparity and its effect on individual freedom. This awareness fostered a critical perspective on societal structures and economic injustices, informing his later literary works with a keen understanding of the human condition in financial adversity.

Amidst the hardships of poverty, Miller found himself drawn to the world of literature and writing, both as a means of escape and as a vehicle for expression. Writing became a refuge, offering solace and a creative outlet in the tumultuous context of financial instability. Her early literary endeavours were woven into the fabric of her daily struggles, intertwining the pursuit of artistic expression with the harsh realities of financial insecurity.

It was while navigating these tumultuous waters that Miller discovered the transformative power of language and narrative, realising the potential to transcend material limitations through writing. It was during this period of financial hardship that Miller's commitment to harnessing the power of literature as a tool for liberation began to take shape, paving the way for her future literary endeavours imbued with a deep understanding of human resilience and the quest for freedom.

Ultimately, Miller's early struggles with financial instability served as a catalyst for his ongoing quest for literary emancipation, pushing him to confront the intertwined complexities of poverty, creativity and freedom. With unwavering determination and a burgeoning passion for literature, he traversed the maze of financial hardship and emerged with a firm resolve to uplift the human spirit through writing.

First steps in writing: Trials and triumphs

Henry Miller's journey as a writer was fraught with difficulties, but it was during these difficult times that he honed his craft and discovered his unique literary voice. Faced with financial instability and societal expectations, Miller forged ahead with an unwavering passion for storytelling. His first attempts at writing were met with scepticism and rejection, but he persevered, delving deeper into the essence of his experiences and emotions.

Miller's unwavering determination led him to experiment with different styles and forms of expression, drawing on the eclectic influences of his past. His writing has become a testament to his resilience, reflecting the raw authenticity of his tumultuous life. Through introspection and analysis, he discovered the profound truths that would later define his work.

In the midst of disillusionment and uncertainty, Miller found solace in the act of creation, embracing the cathartic release that writing provided. His literary pursuits became a sanctuary where he could freely explore the complexities of human existence, unfettered by the constraints of conventional norms. The success and recognition to which he aspired seemed elusive, but his unwavering commitment never wavered.

Triumph emerged from the crucible of adversity, as Miller's unwavering spirit and unstinting dedication bore fruit. The defining moment came when he embarked on a transformative journey to Paris, a city brimming with artistic fervour and intellectual enlightenment. It was there, amidst the vibrant bohemian culture, that Miller met kindred spirits and a supportive community that nurtured his creative endeavours.

It was in the cafés and literary salons of Paris that Miller found validation and inspiration, paving the way for a profound literary awakening. The cobbled streets and enigmatic alleyways served as both backdrop and muse, propelling him towards a new purpose and direction. Paris became the crucible in which Miller's literary identity crystallised, infusing his prose with unbridled power and uninhibited candour.

The trials of his past are transformed into the triumphs of his present, as Miller embraces his vocation with renewed fervour and conviction. From the labyrinthine corridors of self-doubt emerges an emboldened artist, ready to etch an indelible legacy in the annals of literature. This pivotal moment marked the advent of a literary luminary whose unequivocal veracity would reverberate down the generations, forever altering the landscape of modern literature.

From aspirations to expatriation: The trip to Paris

Henry Miller's passion for writing intensified at the same time as his desire for a more liberating environment. In the early 1930s, in the midst of economic and personal turmoil, Miller made a decision that would change the course of his life: he embarked on a transformative journey across the Atlantic to the legendary city of Paris. This move from the far reaches of America to the bohemian haven of Paris symbolised not only a physical displacement, but also a profound ideological shift. It represented a conscious rejection of societal norms and an embrace of unfettered creativity and intellectual exploration.

Arriving in Paris, Miller found himself immersed in a melting pot of artistic expression and cultural diversity. The city exudes the exuberance of creative minds challenging the status quo. From cozy cafés to lively salons, the city offers Miller the perfect setting to hone his craft and meet people who share his thirst for innovation. Lured by the promise of intellectual liberation, he plunged enthusiastically into the tumultuous world of avant-garde literature and provocative philosophical discourse, throwing off the restraints that had stifled him in his homeland.

The attraction of Paris was not limited to its literary and artistic dynamism. For Miller, it was a unique opportunity to embrace life in its rawest form. He revelled in the unbridled atmosphere of Montparnasse, where passions ran wild and inhibitions disappeared. Amid the bustling streets and dimly-lit corners, he encountered a varied humanity that enriched his point of view, fuelling both his writing and his personal development.

Paris has become for Miller not only a geographical destination, but also a metaphorical crossroads, a point of intersection between his ambition and the limitless potential of a city brimming with possibilities. It was a place where he could redefine himself, free himself from the constraints of convention and embrace a profoundly authentic existence. The transformation was palpable, as the convergence of his vision and the spirit of Paris paved the way for his landmark works, which would challenge and redefine the literary landscape.

This convergence gave birth to a narrative that transcended physical boundaries, testifying to the transformative power of an ambitious journey. Miller's time in Paris embodied the essence of an expatriate soul in search of self-discovery and creative fulfilment. It laid the foundations for the bohemian ethos that would permeate his literary endeavours, forever shaping his identity as a writer whose resilience and wanderlust blossomed in the cobbled streets and effervescent culture of a city that dared to defy tradition.

3

Tropic of Cancer

Breaking down boundaries

Introduction to the revolutionary text

Henry Miller's Tropic of Cancer is a testament to the zeitgeist of its time, capturing the essence of a pre-war Paris on the brink of social, political and artistic upheaval. A central figure in the development of modernist literature, Miller imbued his narrative with an unflinching exploration of the human condition, unearthing the raw, unfiltered truths that lurk beneath the facades of society. As an American expatriate, Miller found himself inundated and liberated by the bohemian atmosphere of Paris, where he encountered a milieu of artists, intellectuals and free spirits who collectively rejected the constraints of conventional thinking. It was in this fertile ground of anti-conformism that Tropique du cancer was born, a bold and uninhibited work that shattered literary taboos and boldly challenged established norms.

At its heart, the novel is both a personal exorcism and a scathing indictment of the modern world, transforming introspective reflections into a prophetic critique of civilisation. With unbridled candour, Miller plunges into the depths of human consciousness, embracing the chaotic beauty of existence and defying societal demands for order and restraint. Throughout the text, the reader is intimately invited to witness the revealing journey of an artist actively engaged in dismantling the barriers of traditional morality and conventional literary form. In doing so, Miller pushes the boundaries of the acceptable while fearlessly navigating the tumultuous waters of his own psyche, unmasking the often obscure nuances of desire, despair and disillusionment. Far from being a mere chronicle of his personal endeavours, Tropic of Cancer serves as a manifesto for new modes of expression, encouraging subsequent generations to challenge the status quo and unfurl their own creative banners in defiance of societal repression. This chapter will give readers a better understanding of Miller's underlying motivations and an appreciation of the revolutionary spirit that drives the narrative forward and redefines the very essence of literary art.

Contextualising the period: pre-war Paris

To understand the importance of Henry Miller's seminal work, Tropic of Cancer, it is essential to immerse ourselves in the socio-cultural milieu of pre-war Paris. The inter-war period in Paris was characterised by a bohemian spirit, an atmosphere brimming with intellectual fervour and a sense of liberation from traditional societal constraints. This environment provided fertile ground for artistic experimentation and literary exploration. In the aftermath of the First World War, Paris became a sanctuary for expatriate writers and artists seeking to escape the disillusionment and upheaval that had hit Europe. The influx of creative minds from all over the world fostered an environment of cross-cultural exchange and collaboration, fuelling a climate of freedom and innovation. At the heart of this cultural effervescence was the Montparnasse district, which served as a hub for intellectuals, poets, painters and visionaries.

It was in this lively enclave that Henry Miller found his creative voice and honed his unique artistic vision. The spirit of rebellion and non-conformity permeated the air, fuelling a sense of exhilarating possibility and unbridled creativity. Against this backdrop, Miller's raw, unapologetic prose emerged as a fearless repudiation of societal norms, a bold assertion of individualism and a poignant testament to the human condition. His unflinching portrayal of the underbelly of Parisian life reflects the dissonance and discord that resonate in the city's cobbled alleys and dimly lit cafés. Through vivid, visceral language, Miller has captured the essence of a city on the precipice of profound transformation, a city grappling with its own contradictions and complexities. 'Tropic of Cancer' is a chronicle of this tumultuous time, a testament to the resilient spirit of an avant-garde community that dared to defy convention and embrace the untamed brilliance of the human experience. Thus, the contextualisation of 'Tropic of Cancer' within the dynamic tapestry of pre-war Paris highlights the symbiotic relationship between the artist and the zeitgeist, elucidating the enduring relevance of Miller's magnum opus to the flow of time and evolution.

Breaking literary conventions: style and structure

In Tropic of Cancer, Henry Miller broke the traditional boundaries of literary style and structure, propelling the novel into a realm of unprecedented daring and innovation. Departing from conventional narrative techniques, Miller employed a stream-of-consciousness form that reflected the frantic, tumultuous nature of the protagonist's experiences in bohemian Paris. By forgoing a linear plot progression in favour of a fragmented, anarchic narrative approach, Miller has dismantled the rigid constraints of traditional storytelling, inviting readers to immerse themselves in the raw, unfiltered essence of human existence. This bold departure from established norms not only embodied the spirit of artistic rebellion, but also served as a testament to Miller's unwavering commitment to authenticity and unbridled self-expression.

Moreover, Miller's unorthodox use of language and imagery defies societal expectations and linguistic conventions, freeing the narrative from the shackles of ownership and conformity. Through visceral, uninhibited prose, he fearlessly delved into the darkest recesses of human consciousness, exposing the raw underbelly of emotion, desire and existential angst. His writings, characterised by their immediacy and visceral power, confronted readers with an unvarnished portrait of the human condition, challenging them to confront the uncomfortable truths and profound complexities of life. In doing so, Miller transformed the act of reading into an intrinsically visceral and deeply moving experience, breaking the boundaries of conventional narrative and catapulting literature into uncharted territories of emotional candour and unfettered honesty.

Moreover, the novel's structure, or lack of it, defies established norms, rejecting linearity and coherence in favour of a disorientated but undeniably authentic description of existence. Viewing chaos and disarray as essential components of the human experience, Miller has brazenly thrown off the bounds of traditional narrative, composing a story that echoes the discordant rhythms of life itself. As the contours of the plot blur and the distinction between fact and fiction dissolves, readers are plunged into a maelstrom of uninhibited expression and unfiltered awareness, effectively erasing the boundaries between author, protagonist and audience. This dissolution of structural order encapsulates the fervent desire for artistic liberation, reflecting Miller's unwavering commitment to subverting literary conventions and embracing the wild landscapes of creativity and individuality.

The protagonist: Henry as antagonist

In Tropic of Cancer, Henry Miller's character does not emerge as the hero par excellence, but rather as an antagonist to conventional norms and societal expectations. Henry, the semi-autobiographical protagonist, embodies a complex mix of raw honesty, carnal desire and uncompromising rebellion. Depicted through his radical perspectives and unfiltered confessions, Henry challenges the traditional portrayal of a protagonist, seeking truth in the midst of decay and chaos.

Henry's antagonistic nature is evident in his relentless pursuit of individuality, often at the expense of social acceptance. Freed from moral constraints, he plunges into the depths of human experience, confronting taboo subjects with a frankness that defies censorship and raises fundamental questions about the very nature of morality. His actions and thoughts serve as a catalyst to redefine the role of the protagonist, setting aside archetypal virtues and embracing the complexity of human desires and flaws.

Moreover, Henry's antagonism extends beyond personal boundaries to encompass the very fabric of society, challenging established institutions and exposing their inherent hypocrisies. Through his rebellious spirit and unwavering authenticity, Henry becomes a symbolic figure embodying disillusionment with the status quo, inspiring readers to embark on their own quest for self-discovery and liberation.

The embodiment of the anti-hero, Henry's antagonistic presence enriches the narrative with a multifaceted exploration of human contradictions and existential struggles. His character serves as a mirror reflecting the inner turmoil and unconventional aspirations that lurk beneath the veneer of societal conformity, forcing readers to confront the dichotomies of their own existence and embrace the complexities of the human experience.

Ultimately, Henry's role as antagonist transcends the confines of the fictional narrative and resonates as a provocative emblem of defiance and autonomy. By opposing convention and moral absolutism, Henry challenges readers to re-evaluate their perception of virtue and vice, celebrating the intrinsic discordance that defines the human condition. In doing so, he left an indelible mark on the literary landscape, inviting audiences to confront the uncomfortable truths and unsettling beauty of a world marked by contradiction.

Love, lust and liberation: challenging morality

In the vibrant tapestry of Tropique du Cancer, love, lust and liberation converge to challenge conventional morality and societal norms. Henry Miller's unflinching portrayal of carnal desire and the subtleties of human relationships transcends the boundaries of traditional literary representations, offering an unflinching exploration of the complexities of human desire and the quest for individual freedom. At its core, this candid tale elucidates the tumultuous interplay between passion, intimacy and the deep-seated societal constraints that seek to suppress the raw expression of human emotion. Miller's unabashed approach not only defies conventional morality, but also serves as a metaphorical call to arms, urging readers to embrace their primal instincts and free themselves from the shackles of societal expectations. The evocative description of libidinous encounters in the bohemian enclaves of Paris serves as a rebellion against Puritan ideologies, fostering a profound sense of liberation in both characters and readers.

In these pages, moral boundaries are tested, dismantled and ultimately reconstructed, giving rise to a new appreciation of the spectrum of human emotions and experiences. The unvarnished exploration of love and lust in Tropic of Cancer not only challenges societal morality, but also fosters a deeper understanding of the multifaceted nature of human relationships, transcending the boundaries of normative standards and embracing the complexity inherent in our emotional landscape. By confronting and subverting conventional moral ideals, Miller's story becomes a powerful channel for introspection, prompting readers to re-evaluate their perceptions of love, sex and freedom in a society that often seeks to limit their expression. As the story unfolds, the juxtaposition of unbridled passion and societal repression unleashes a poignant discourse on the fundamental rights of individuals to pursue unbridled happiness and fulfilment. Through unparalleled prose and unflinching narrative, Miller invites readers to confront the uncomfortable truths of human desire, challenging the very essence of imposed morality and inspiring a collective re-examination of the boundaries that confine our deepest aspirations.

Writers and artists: Representations of the creative underworld

In 'Tropique du cancer', Henry Miller vividly depicts the bohemian lifestyle and creative world of 1930s Paris. This section explores the rich tapestry of writers and artists who populate the novel, offering a glimpse into their unconventional lives and artistic pursuits. Miller's raw, unabashed prose introduces readers to a group of characters who defy societal norms and revel in their individuality. Through his descriptions, Miller captures the essence of the 'starving artist' archetype, depicting individuals driven by passion and artistic vision, often at the expense of conventional success. The novel brings to life the cafés, salons and street corners where these creatives gather, exchanging ideas, challenging each other and engaging in lively discussions about art, literature and the human experience. From struggling poets to eccentric painters, Miller paints a vivid and sometimes chaotic portrait of the creative community, highlighting both its vitality and its difficulties.

Through gripping anecdotes and larger-than-life personalities, Miller immerses the reader in a world where passion takes precedence over material comfort, and where art is a way of life rather than a profession. Miller's portrait also challenges romanticised notions of the artist's life, presenting a raw, unvarnished view of the sacrifices and joys that accompany creative endeavour. In doing so, he blurs the line between fiction and reality, drawing on his own experiences and observations to create a compelling and authentic portrait of the creative underworld. Readers are invited to witness the exhilarating highs and crushing lows experienced by the inhabitants of this vibrant and turbulent milieu. Ultimately, 'Tropic of Cancer' is a captivating testament to the enduring appeal and challenge of the creative spirit, as well as a poignant exploration of the human condition in all its complexity.

Candid Confessions: Autobiographical Elements

In the raw, unabashed prose of Tropic of Cancer, Henry Miller unearths a deeply personal narrative that blurs the boundaries between fiction and autobiography. Its protagonist, the fervently honest and irreverent Henry, becomes the vessel for Miller's existential experiences, beliefs and reflections. Entering the nooks and crannies of Miller's world, readers discover candid explorations of his relationships, struggles and relentless quest for emancipation from societal constraints. Through the provocative, unfiltered lens of his alter ego, Miller reveals intimate revelations about love, sex, mortality and the quest for artistic truth. It is in these pages of confession that the reader gains access to the inner sanctum of Miller's thoughts and desires. This uncompromising self-examination, interwoven with poignant and exuberant moments, offers a profound insight into the author's psyche and testifies to his uncompromising commitment to authenticity.

Through unvarnished revelations and autobiographical reflections, 'Tropic of Cancer' transcends the label of mere fiction and stands as a bold memoir of one man's unwavering odyssey of self-discovery. By interweaving his own story with that of the novel's protagonist, Miller forces readers to confront the universal truths and complexities of the human condition, laying bare the turbulent terrain of his own life with an unvarnished sincerity that provokes both reflection and admiration. Navigating the intricate web of personal revelations and introspective reflections, the reader is invited into the recesses of Henry Miller's being and in turn finds himself immersed in a literary portrait that pulsates with the brilliance and intensity of a life lived unfettered. The candour with which Miller shares his triumphs and tribulations gives 'Tropic of Cancer' an unparalleled depth and emotional resonance, forging an unbreakable bond between author and audience and cementing its status as a seminal work that transcends genres and eras.

Critical reception: Initial indignation and subsequent acclaim

Henry Miller's Tropic of Cancer provoked controversy and intense reaction when it was first published in 1934. The raw, unfiltered depiction of sexuality, combined with explicit language and a frank exploration of taboo subjects, unleashed a storm of indignation in literary and moral circles. Critics and authorities condemned the book as obscene and morally depraved, leading to widespread censorship and bans in many countries, including the United States, where the book was the subject of legal challenges and not widely distributed until the 1960s.

The visceral reaction to Tropic of Cancer reflected the deep-rooted societal taboos and moral boundaries that prevailed during the inter-war years. Miller's uncompromising portrayal of human desire, disillusionment and existential angst confronted readers with an unvarnished view of life's complexities, challenging established norms and provoking unease among those entrenched in traditional values. The controversy surrounding the novel propelled it into public discourse, sparking debates about the limits of artistic expression and the role of literature in reflecting and questioning the mores of society.

Despite the initial furore and repression, Tropic of Cancer eventually transcended its tumultuous reception to become widely acclaimed and recognised for its literary merits and profound ideas. Over time, fervent opposition gave way to critical reappraisal and a new appreciation of the novel's revolutionary narrative style and its unreserved embrace of human experience. Scholars and literary commentators have praised Miller's work for its bold experimentation with form, its unwavering authenticity and its courageous denunciation of society's hypocrisy and pretence.

The changing attitudes towards Tropic of Cancer reflect wider cultural shifts that challenge repressive attitudes and celebrate individual freedom and artistic autonomy. As society evolved to embrace more liberal perspectives on sexuality and expression, Miller's once-vilified opus received renewed attention and respect, heralding a renaissance in its critical reception and establishing its enduring status as a seminal work of twentieth-century literature. Tropic of Cancer's journey from condemnation to canonisation testifies to the transformative power of art and the enduring appeal of provocative and daring literary creations.

The battles of censorship: The fight for freedom of expression

Throughout literary history, certain works have challenged societal norms and pushed back the boundaries of artistic expression. Henry Miller's Tropic of Cancer is one of these monumental texts that has been subject to scrutiny and censorship battles in its quest for freedom of expression. From its first publication in 1934 to subsequent reprints and translations, the novel has been at the centre of numerous legal and cultural conflicts. The explicit language, unabashed depiction of sexuality and raw description of human experience constituted a direct challenge to prevailing moral standards, and this provoked vehement opposition from conservative circles and the authorities.

For decades, Tropic of Cancer was banned in several countries, including the United States, where it was the subject of obscenity lawsuits and legal restrictions. This situation gave rise to fervent debate about the limits of artistic licence and the role of literature in confronting uncomfortable truths. Defenders of the novel have defended its right to exist within the realm of free speech and artistic expression, while its detractors have sought to suppress its dissemination, fearing its potential impact on the mores of society. The dichotomy between artistic freedom and public decency has become the focal point of these censorship battles, sparking profound discussions about the power dynamics between creators, regulators and consumers of literature.

The perseverance of publishers, artists and advocates ultimately led to significant advances in challenging censorship laws and repressive attitudes towards provocative literature. Historic legal victories and changing cultural attitudes gradually eroded the barriers that had prevented the unfettered circulation of Tropic of Cancer and other controversial works. These efforts not only secured the novel's place in the literary canon, but also contributed to broader movements advocating freedom of expression in various art forms. The lasting impact of Tropic of Cancer's battles against censorship resonates beyond the confines of literature, testifying to the indomitable spirit of creative expression and the ongoing struggle for artistic autonomy in the face of societal resistance.

A lasting impact: a catalyst for change

The lasting impact of Tropic of Cancer extends far beyond its initial publication and into the tumultuous censorship battles that characterised its early years. Miller's explicit prose and unflinching depiction of human desire met with strong opposition, with bans and legal challenges preventing the book's distribution. However, this resistance only served to reinforce the novel's mystique and consolidate its position as a literary touchstone in the realm of artistic freedom and expression.

Decades after its controversial release, Tropique du cancer continues to serve as a catalyst for change and an example of literature's ability to challenge societal norms. Its unflinching portrayal of sexuality, existentialism and rebellion against traditional morality reverberates across generations, influencing subsequent authors and inspiring readers to confront the complexities of the human condition with unwavering honesty and introspection.

Miller's bold challenge to literary and societal conventions ushered in an era of unparalleled creative freedom, ushering in a new wave of literature that pushed boundaries and encouraged discourse on the limits of art and expression. Today, Tropic of Cancer remains a testament to the enduring power of literature to provoke, enlighten and incite change.

Moreover, Tropic of Cancer's relevance is underlined by its continued resonance in societal conversations about censorship, freedom of expression and evolving definitions of obscenity. While debates about artistic freedoms persist, Miller's work remains a cornerstone, reminding audiences of the unwavering importance of defending the right to create and consume art without undue restriction.

In classrooms, libraries and cultural debates around the world, Tropic of Cancer is seen as a transformative force, prompting readers to question the essence of human desire, ambition and the relentless pursuit of individual freedom. Its legacy fosters a better understanding of historical struggles for artistic autonomy, while inspiring contemporary efforts to dismantle barriers to unrestricted artistic expression.

Ultimately, Tropic of Cancer endures not only as a novel, but also as an emblem of the resilience, tenacity and enduring influence of literature on the collective consciousness. Its lasting impact as a catalyst for change is an indelible testament to literature's enduring power to transcend time, provoke critical discourse and shape the socio-cultural landscape.

4

Parisian Muse

The City of Liberation

Paris in the early 20th century

At the beginning of the 20th century, Paris was a crucible of artistic and intellectual revolution, a magnetic centre that attracted creative minds from all over the world. The city bubbled with electrifying energy as artists, writers and thinkers sought refuge in its bohemian quarters, each seeking inspiration and liberation from the norms and traditions of society.

The cultural landscape of Paris at this time was a tumultuous but fertile ground for innovation. Avant-garde movements such as Cubism, Surrealism, Dadaism and Existentialism were flourishing, challenging conventional artistic and philosophical paradigms. The city's eclectic neighbourhoods, such as Montmartre and Montparnasse, were home to a vibrant expatriate community, fostering an atmosphere conducive to collaboration and boundary-pushing creativity.

At the heart of this creative fervour is the appeal of the freedom and self-expression that Paris offers. For many expatriate artists and writers, Paris represented a sanctuary where they could freely explore their art without the constraints imposed by the conservatism that prevailed in their home countries. This environment of artistic and existential liberation attracted such luminaries as Pablo Picasso, Gertrude Stein, James Joyce and Ernest Hemingway, who all converged on the banks of the Seine, each contributing to the vibrant tapestry of cultural exchange and influence.

Moreover, in the early twentieth century, Paris was not just a physical place, but a state of mind - a bohemian ethos that permeated every cobbled street and dimly lit café. Here, unconventional ideas flowed freely, fuelled by the passionate debates and discussions that took place in the city's many meeting places. Iconic venues such as the Café de Flore, Les Deux Magots and La Rotonde became melting pots of intellectual effervescence, where polemicists, poets and painters gathered to exchange radical ideas and experiments.

This period in Parisian history bears witness to the lasting impact of cultural exchange on creative expression, embodying a harmonious interweaving of national identities in a collective, cosmopolitan spirit. The ensuing crossroads of diverse artistic currents provided the impetus for new forms of expression, captivated by the relentless pursuit of innovation and unbridled freedom of thought.

Paris became a canvas on which the colours of human passion, intellect and creativity converged, blending harmoniously to compose a symphony of revolutionary art and literature. The next chapters will delve deeper into the profound influences this remarkable environment exerted on Henry Miller's life and work, highlighting how the spirit of Paris in the early twentieth century shaped his transformative journey as a writer and visionary.

The lure of expatriate life: A haven for writers

Throughout the 20th century, Paris attracted a multitude of expatriate artists and writers seeking to escape the constraints of their home countries. The lure of expatriate life in Paris allowed individuals like Henry Miller to break free from societal norms and explore their creative impulses without inhibition. The cosmopolitan atmosphere, rich cultural tapestry and liberal attitudes towards art and literature attracted a vibrant expatriate community, fostering an environment conducive to artistic exploration and expression.

For Miller, Paris symbolised freedom, both personal and creative, offering an escape from the moral rigidity and censorship that prevailed in the United States between the wars. He found himself immersed in a melting pot of cultures and ideologies, invigorated by the city's intellectual ferment and unbridled spirit. Expatriate circles provided an invaluable support network, allowing Miller to meet writers and artists who shared his passion for pushing the boundaries of conventional expression. Surrounded by kindred spirits, he was able to throw off the constraints of traditional literary conventions and embrace the unvarnished reality of existence. The bohemian lifestyle of the expatriate community infused Miller's work with a raw, uninhibited energy that resonated with readers and other writers.

In the heart of Montparnasse, where creativity flowed as freely as wine, Miller found solace and camaraderie in the company of visionaries and free thinkers who celebrated the complexities of life with fervour and authenticity. The experience of expatriating to Paris offered Miller the opportunity to redefine his identity, free from the constraints of the past and the expectations imposed by conservative societies. Here, amid the winding streets and elegant boulevards, he discovered a sense of belonging that transcended national boundaries, embracing the universal language of human expression. Paris became more than just a backdrop for Miller's literary endeavours; it became an integral part of his artistic evolution, shaping his vision of the world and enriching his prose with a depth and vitality born of passionate self-discovery. The appeal of expatriate life in Paris lay not only in its physical beauty, but also in its ability to ignite the creative spark in those who sought refuge in its enchanting embrace.

Cafés and conversations: intellectual encounters

In the early twentieth century, Parisian cafés were hotbeds of intellectual exchange, where writers, artists and thinkers gathered for in-depth discussion and debate. They were essential meeting places for literary minds to exchange ideas, challenge convention and find inspiration in the company of like-minded individuals. Within this vibrant café culture, Henry Miller found himself immersed in lively discourse and wonderful company, each encounter leaving an indelible mark on the evolution of his worldview and creative endeavours.

One of these emblematic establishments is the Café de Flore, a renowned haunt of literary luminaries and philosophers. It was here, amid the heady aromas of coffee and cigarette smoke, that Miller would engage in passionate debates and unfiltered conversations with his fellow expatriates, touching on subjects ranging from existentialism to the nature of art. These exchanges often went on late into the night, amid the ambient hum of voices and clinking glasses, helping to create an atmosphere brimming with intellectual energy.

Another famous venue was Les Deux Magots, where Miller would meet kindred spirits such as Anaïs Nin, challenging and enriching each other's perspectives through frank dialogue. The attraction of these meetings lay not only in the exchange of ideas, but also in the diversity of viewpoints and experiences that converged within the hallowed walls of these establishments. It was there, in the bohemian atmosphere, that Miller found himself enmeshed in a network of relationships that fuelled his creativity and strengthened his commitment to artistic expression in its purest form.

The café scene is also fertile ground for chance encounters and unexpected collaborations. It was in these sacred places that Miller forged lasting friendships with painters, poets and visionaries who shared his quest for personal and artistic freedom. Their collective presence imbued the air with an electric charge, igniting the spark of inspiration that would light Miller's literary path.

In retrospect, these intellectual symposia underscore the essential role that Parisian cafés played in shaping Miller's literary sensibility and his determination to defy conventional norms. They offered him a sanctuary where unbridled creativity and radical ideas flourished, blossoming amidst the rich tapestry of intellect and imagination woven by the diverse individuals who sought refuge in these venerable institutions.

The influence of Surrealism

The Surrealist movement, with its emphasis on the unconscious, dream imagery and spontaneous creativity, exerted a profound influence on literary and artistic circles in Paris in the early twentieth century. For Henry Miller, the encounter with Surrealist ideas and techniques was a catalytic experience that left an indelible mark on his writing and his vision of the world. Surrealism radically challenged conventional artistic norms and set out to unravel the mysteries of the human psyche. Immersing himself in this intellectual milieu, Miller found himself drawn to the Surrealist concept of automatic writing, which emphasised the unfiltered expression of thoughts and emotions without the constraints of conscious control. This liberation from traditional literary forms and structures allowed Miller to tap into the raw, primal energy of his innermost thoughts and experiences, resulting in a distinctive, uninhibited prose style characteristic of his later work.

The Surrealists' fascination with the subconscious and the irrational resonates deeply with Miller's own exploration of existential themes and the complexities of human existence. The fusion of surrealist principles with his unique vision allowed him to cross the boundaries of conventional storytelling, creating a narrative terrain where the strange and the mundane coexist harmoniously. Moreover, the surrealist preoccupation with the absurd and the fantastic dovetails perfectly with Miller's penchant for vivid, visceral descriptions and bold, often surprising imagery, giving his writing a hypnotic, dreamlike quality that defies easy categorisation. Moreover, the subversive and rebellious spirit of Surrealism reflected Miller's own ethos of defying social convention and artistic orthodoxy, encouraging him to fearlessly defy prevailing norms and embrace the wildness of his creative impulses. Indeed, the influence of Surrealism on Miller's literary development cannot be overstated; it provided him with a rich tapestry of conceptual and stylistic innovation, guiding him towards an ever-deeper engagement with the enigmatic depths of human consciousness and the perplexing theatre of existence itself.

Personal liberation and cultural exploration

Amidst the bohemian allure of Paris, Henry Miller found himself immersed in a whirlwind of personal liberation and cultural exploration. The city's open-mindedness and artistic effervescence provided the perfect backdrop for Miller's journey of self-discovery. Freed from the constraints imposed by American societal norms, Miller embraced the freedom to explore his own identity and philosophy unfettered. With each cobbled street and encounter with creative colleagues, he delved deeper into the vast expanse of personal expression.

Embracing the multicultural tapestry of Paris, Miller engaged with a diverse community that transcended geographical boundaries. His interactions with artists, writers and thinkers from around the world enriched his understanding of different cultures and perspectives. Through these relationships, Miller broadened his intellectual horizons and cultivated a deep appreciation for the interconnectedness of the human experience. This deep immersion in a cutting-edge environment enabled her to challenge preconceptions and traditional values, fostering a heightened sense of compassion and empathy.

In this environment of relentless creativity, Miller became involved in the Surrealist movement, drawing inspiration from the subconscious and the unconventional. Surrealism's emphasis on the irrational and disturbing resonated with his own quest for artistic authenticity and unbridled expression. As he navigates the enigmatic landscapes of his own psyche, Miller's writing takes on an introspective, dreamlike quality, reflecting the influence of Surrealism on his literary pursuits.

Moreover, the freedom of expression within this avant-garde community encouraged Miller to push back the boundaries of conventional thought and engage in radical experimentation. He defied societal norms with his uninhibited approach to life and love, echoing the fervent ethic of liberation that permeated Parisian artistic circles. This era of personal and artistic freedom influenced his later work, infusing it with an uninhibited spirit that defied censorship and convention.

Miller's Parisian sojourn triggered a period of transformation, self-realisation and cross-cultural assimilation. Personalities from disparate backgrounds converged in a melting pot of creativity, contributing to the visceral tapestry of Miller's experiences. His exploration of the self and engagement with diverse cultural landscapes underscore the importance of Paris as a catalyst for personal development and introspection.

An avant-garde community: friends and collaborators

Henry Miller's time in Paris was profoundly enriched by the vibrant community of fellow writers, artists and intellectuals who gathered in the city's exuberant atmosphere. Among them was Anaïs Nin, writer and diarist, whose relationship with Miller was both creative and personal. The two women shared a deep intellectual and emotional bond, and their exchange of ideas and experiences shaped their respective works. Their correspondence and mutual exploration of themes such as freedom, love and creativity added a layer of depth to Miller's literary projects.

In addition to Nin, Miller found himself in the company of like-minded, convention-defying individuals who embraced the bohemian spirit of the time. These companions, often expatriates themselves, brought diverse perspectives from different corners of the world, fostering an environment of cultural exchange and creative cross-pollination. Miller engaged in lively debates, dialogues and collaborative projects with this avant-garde circle, forging lasting friendships that would leave an indelible mark on his writing.

The collective energy of this community inspired Miller to challenge existing literary norms and embark on ambitious artistic projects. The camaraderie and support of his contemporaries comforted him in times of personal and professional adversity, strengthening his resolve to pursue his unorthodox vision despite external scepticism and hardship.

Beyond his intellectual and artistic activities, these relationships also played a crucial role in shaping Miller's worldview and philosophical outlook. Discussions of existentialism, human nature and the search for truth permeated the meetings, serving as fertile ground for his contemplations and explorations. Within this social milieu, Miller developed a sense of belonging and camaraderie that transcended geographical boundaries and temporal constraints.

Moreover, the spirit of collaboration within this community extended beyond intellectual discourse, resulting in joint projects and interdisciplinary artistic experiments. These collective endeavours fuelled Miller's creative fire, opening up new possibilities for expression and pushing back the boundaries of traditional art forms.

Ultimately, the dynamic network of friendships and collaborations in Paris not only elevated Miller's artistic endeavours, but also deepened his understanding of the human condition, enriching his literary legacy with a tapestry of influences and experiences that continue to resonate with readers across generations.

Struggles and triumphs: Overcoming difficulties

Henry Miller's stay in Paris was not without its difficulties. Despite the allure of bohemia, he faced many difficulties that tested his resolve and determination. Financial difficulties were a constant companion, with Miller often living hand-to-mouth, taking menial jobs to support his artistic activities. The pressures of poverty and uncertainty weighed heavily on him, but he found solace in the camaraderie of fellow artists and thinkers who shared his unconventional ideals.

The formidable task of navigating a foreign culture and language has added another layer of complexity to Miller's experience. As an expatriate, he was confronted with feelings of isolation and alienation, with the ever-present sense of being an outsider. However, this sense of displacement ultimately fuelled his creative spirit, giving him a fresh perspective on the world around him.

In the midst of these difficulties, Miller persevered, finding inspiration in the vibrant tapestry of Parisian life. In the face of adversity, he channelled his experiences into his writing, using his observations and personal trials to fuel his literary endeavours. His steadfast dedication to his craft and unwavering faith in his artistic vision enabled him to transcend obstacles and emerge stronger and more resilient.

Triumphs punctuated this arduous journey, marking important milestones in Miller's artistic and personal evolution. By dint of determination and indomitability, he carved out a place for himself on the avant-garde literary scene, gaining recognition for his unique voice and his unabashed exploration of taboo subjects.

Ultimately, the hardships endured in Paris served as essential catalysts for Miller's growth, shaping his identity as a writer and influencing the themes that would define his work. The dichotomy of struggle and triumph wove a rich tapestry of experience, contributing to the multifaceted nature of Miller's legacy and cementing his indelible mark on the literary landscape.

Paris in literature: Inspiration from the urban landscape

Navigating the bustling streets and quiet alleys of Paris, Henry Miller found himself enveloped in a city that exuded art, literature and history. The mere presence of iconic monuments such as the Eiffel Tower, Notre Dame Cathedral and the Louvre Museum fired his imagination, offering endless possibilities for narrative and introspection. Every cobbled street whispered stories of revolution, romance and resilience, fostering a deep connection between the city and Miller's literary exploration. From the grandeur of the Champs-Élysées to the intimacy of Montmartre, Paris served as both muse and mentor, shaping Miller's prose with its rich tapestry of experiences and stories. The contrasting landscapes of the Seine and bustling markets awakened his senses, imbuing his work with the vibrant imagery and energy characteristic of the City of Light.

Henry Miller's time in Paris played an essential role in the development of his philosophical ideas. Immersed in the city's rich cultural tapestry, Miller was exposed to a diversity of thought that profoundly influenced his intellectual development. The lively streets of Montparnasse and the bohemian atmosphere of the Left Bank provided fertile ground for Miller to explore existential themes and adopt a more liberated outlook on life.

In Paris, Miller met thinkers and artists who challenged traditional norms and conventions, pushing the boundaries of creative expression and philosophical inquiry. The city's vibrant intellectual community fostered an environment in which Miller could engage with avant-garde ideas and forge his own path as a writer, unbound by societal constraints.

The existential currents of Parisian life seeped into Miller's consciousness, prompting him to introspect and re-evaluate his place in the world. The juxtaposition of luxury and poverty, freedom and restriction, left an indelible imprint on Miller's worldview, shaping his fundamental beliefs about the human condition and the search for authenticity.

Paris also served as a catalyst for Miller's exploration of sensuality and spirituality, interweaving the physical and metaphysical dimensions of existence. The city's architectural marvels and effervescent energy inspired Miller to delve into the realms of love, desire and transcendence, weaving these profound experiences into the fabric of his literary works.

Navigating the labyrinthine alleys and labyrinthine human interactions of Paris, Miller was confronted with questions of identity, purpose and moral autonomy. The city's contradictions became the crucible for his philosophical reflections, pushing him to confront the complexities of human nature and the enigma of personal freedom.

Ultimately, the transformative power of Paris manifested itself in the maturation of Miller's philosophical vision, infusing his writings with unparalleled depth and nuance. Every cobbled street and dimly lit café became a canvas for Miller's contemplations, paving the way for the profound ideas that would permeate his literary work and resonate with generations of readers. Paris, in all its complexity, became the backdrop for Miller's philosophical evolution, leaving an indelible mark on his work forever.

The legacy of a city: the long-term impact on Miller's work

Henry Miller's literary legacy is inexorably linked to the city of Paris. The imprint of this dynamic metropolis on Miller's work extends far beyond the temporal limits of his physical presence in the city. Paris has become an enduring muse that continues to inspire and influence Miller's work long after he has left its cobbled streets. The essence of Paris, as internalized by Miller, permeates his writing, infusing it with a palpable sense of liberation and unfettered creativity.

The lasting impact of Paris on Miller's work goes beyond mere geographical boundaries; rather, it is a profound and enduring spiritual influence that underpins the ethos of his literary production. Miller's engagement with the avant-garde community of Paris catalysed a transformative evolution in his artistic expression. The city exposed him to a rich tapestry of cultural, intellectual and philosophical influences that permeated his work, giving it a particular depth and richness. Paris acted as a crucible for Miller's thoughts and ideas, providing fertile ground for the germination of his idiosyncratic vision of the world. Every cobbled street, smoky café and bohemian enclave left an indelible impression on Miller's creative consciousness, shaping the very fabric of his literary identity.

The legacy of Paris is perceptible in the fluidity and uninhibited nature of Miller's prose, characterised by a raw, unabashed exploration of the human condition. Moreover, the city's cosmopolitan dynamism has infused Miller's writing with a global perspective, transcending the confines of parochialism to embrace a universal relevance that resonates across time and space. The enduring legacy of Paris on Miller's work testifies to the enduring appeal and magnetic influence of this cultural epicentre. Although Miller's physical sojourn in Paris has faded from memory, the city continued to inhabit the inner landscapes of his imagination, fostering a sustained dialogue between the writer and his muse. This enduring legacy is a poignant testament to the transformative power of place in shaping artistic sensibilities, perpetuating the myth of Paris as a crucible of boundless inspiration and creative potential.

5

The Art of Chaos

Crafting Tropic of Capricorn

Introduction to chaos and form

The concept of chaos as a literary process has profound implications for form in literature, challenging traditional structures and inviting readers to reconsider the very essence of narrative. As an elemental force that defies order and predictability, chaos reveals the raw, unfiltered realities of human existence, reflecting the tumultuous nature of life itself. In literature, chaos serves as a catalyst for narrative exploration, destabilising conventional frameworks to reveal deeper truths about the human experience.

By harnessing the inherent disorder of chaos, writers can infuse their works with unparalleled dynamism and authenticity, inviting readers to confront the raw, untamed energy that drives characters and plot. The disruptive influence of chaos pushes back the boundaries of form, providing fertile ground for creative experimentation and innovation. In this maelstrom of unpredictability, traditional narrative structures are challenged, encouraging authors to create narratives that reflect the complex, non-linear paths of human consciousness. This break with linearity gives authors the freedom to construct narratives that better reflect the fluid and complex nature of lived experience. By adopting chaos as a central thematic element, authors can weave rich tapestries of interconnected events and emotions, capturing the ineffable interplay of fate, choice and chance in the human journey.

Chaos offers authors the opportunity to subvert traditional notions of resolution and closure, allowing stories to culminate not in neat resolutions, but in poignant reflection on life's enduring enigmas. In the hands of great storytellers, chaos becomes a powerful tool for evoking visceral and emotional responses from readers, immersing them in the raw intensity of human struggle, triumph and revelation. Ultimately, the introduction of chaos as a literary device encourages writers to break the boundaries of form, allowing them to sculpt narratives that pulsate with undeniable vitality and immediacy, transcending the constraints of traditional storytelling. Indeed, through the harmonious coalescence of chaos and form, literature achieves a transformative power, inviting readers to engage with narratives that resonate at a deep and primal level.

Contextualisation of Tropic of Capricorn: historical and personal context

Henry Miller's Tropic of Capricorn, a landmark work in the literary canon, is inextricably linked to the author's historical and personal context. To fully understand the depth and importance of the novel, it is imperative to immerse oneself in the historical milieu in which Miller navigated. The early twentieth century witnessed seismic shifts in societal norms, upheavals and the disintegration of traditional values, creating an environment conducive to artistic rebellion and redefinition.

This tumultuous backdrop, encompassing economic depression, geopolitical upheaval and social flux, formed the cultural landscape in which

Miller set his narrative. At the same time, Miller's personal journey, marked by wandering, bohemian ideals and an unwavering quest for individuality, significantly shaped the thematic undercurrents of Tropic of Capricorn. His experience of life among the marginalised, the deprived and the outcast is the source of the gritty realism that permeates the novel, illustrating a stark reflection of the human condition.

Miller's intimate exploration of his own psyche, conflicts and ambitions has seeped into the prose, infusing it with a raw, unapologetic authenticity. By placing Tropic of Capricorn in the context of this historical and personal tapestry, readers gain a deep understanding of the confluence of external influences and internal struggles that gave birth to this unparalleled literary work. The fusion of a tumultuous era and an individual odyssey coalesce over the pages, underscoring the interconnectedness of art and life, as well as the enduring relevance of Miller's introspective discourse.

Innovative storytelling: breaking with conventional narrative

Henry Miller's Tropic of Capricorn bears witness to the author's rebellion against conventional narrative techniques. In this profound work, Miller defies traditional narrative structures, opting instead for a raw, unfiltered stream of consciousness that reflects the chaos and complexity of human existence. Through a non-linear and fragmented narrative, Miller paints a vivid and unflinching portrait of his experiences, making a radical departure from the linear, plot-driven narrative prevalent in literature. The novel transports readers into a world where time is fluid, memories intertwine with present experiences, and the boundaries between reality and imagination become blurred. This bold approach encourages readers to engage with the text on a more visceral and emotional level, inviting them to embrace the messiness inherent in life.

Miller's innovative stories capture the essence of human experience in its rawest form, highlighting the many facets of existence and the often contradictory aspects of the human psyche. Through his non-conformist narratives, Miller exposes the fractured and multi-layered nature of reality, forcing readers to confront the messy and paradoxical truths that define our lives. The novel's structure reflects the chaotic rhythms of existence, refusing to provide neat resolutions or conclusions. Instead, it plunges the reader into the whirlpool of the protagonist's consciousness, immersing him or her in a world of visceral, unfiltered emotions and thoughts.

By subverting established literary conventions, Miller invites readers to embrace the messiness of human experience, challenging them to abandon preconceived notions of narrative and immerse themselves in the tangled web of human existence. Thanks to this innovative narrative style, Tropic of Capricorn transcends the boundaries of traditional storytelling, offering a profound and unflinchingly honest portrait of the discord and unpredictability inherent in life. Navigating the fragmented landscape of Miller's prose, the reader is confronted with the full range of human emotions and experiences, from exhilarating highs to heartbreaking lows, from profound insights to existential uncertainties. The innovative stories in Tropic of Capricorn serve as a catalyst for readers to re-evaluate their understanding of the narrative itself, encouraging them to embrace the fractures and complexities inherent in the human condition.

Thematic explorations: The essence of the human experience

In Tropic of Capricorn, Henry Miller delves into thematic explorations of the essence of the human experience, presenting a raw and unflinching examination of the human condition. Through vivid and unfiltered descriptions of the characters and their interactions, Miller confronts the complexities of love, desire and the relentless search for meaning in a world filled with chaos and disorder. The novel explores the paradoxes of human nature, depicting the struggle for authenticity amidst societal constraints and personal uncertainties.

Miller's exploration of the human experience goes beyond the individual to encompass wider social and cultural dynamics. He scrutinises the fabric of society, exposing its hypocrisies and injustices while celebrating the resilience and spirit of the marginalised and oppressed. Through this lens, he unravels the tapestry of human experience, revealing the interconnectedness of joy and sadness, hope and despair, and the fragile interplay of light and darkness in humanity's collective narrative.

Moreover, Tropic of Capricorn's thematic explorations traverse the realms of existentialism and the search for meaning in a seemingly absurd and indifferent universe. Miller tackles questions of purpose and existence, challenging conventional notions of success, fulfilment and identity. His profound reflections on the human psyche and the universal quest for meaning resonate viscerally with readers, prompting them to introspect and contemplate their own life experiences.

The novel also explores the subtleties of human relationships, highlighting the nuances of love, intimacy and human connection. With unflinching honesty, Miller depicts the fragility and beauty of human bonds, imbued with moments of tenderness, passion and disillusionment. Through these thematic explorations, Tropic of Capricorn transcends simple narrative and becomes a profound meditation on the complexities of the human experience.

Ultimately, Miller invites readers to confront the fundamental truths of human existence, embracing the inherent contradictions and ambiguities that define our humanity. With its bold and incisive thematic explorations, Tropic of Capricorn stands as a timeless testament to the richness and tumultuousness of the human journey, compelling us to confront our vulnerabilities, celebrate our resilience and engage with the deep tapestry of human experience.

Stylistic elements: Language as a metaphor for the messiness of life

In Tropic of Capricorn, Henry Miller masterfully employs stylistic elements that intricately reflect the disorder and tumultuous nature of life. In his prose, Miller imbues language with a hypnotic energy that reflects the chaotic essence of human existence. The disjointed, rhythmic flow of his writing captures the frenetic pace of modern life, reflecting the fragmented nature of human experience. This deliberate fragmentation is a powerful metaphor for the disarray and unpredictability inherent in the human condition. Miller employs a raw, unabashed tone, using vivid imagery to convey the raw emotions and conflicts that permeate the characters' lives. In so doing, he invites readers into a world where the boundaries between order and chaos become blurred, highlighting the complexity of the human psyche.
Miller's linguistic playfulness and disregard for conventional grammatical norms serve to challenge literary conventions and disrupt reader expectations. By incorporating slang, foreign phrases and colloquialisms into his narrative, Miller creates a rich tapestry of linguistic diversity that reflects the many facets of society. In addition, the seamless integration of philosophical and introspective reflections adds depth to the narrative, offering a profound insight into the tumultuous landscapes of the human soul. As a result, Miller's stylistic choices not only capture the messiness of life, they also invite readers to confront the existential paradoxes and contradictions that define the human experience. Ultimately, 'Tropic of Capricorn' is a testament to Miller's mastery of language as a means of expressing the complexities and discordances of life, leaving an indelible mark on the literary landscape.

Character studies: The protagonists and their dualities

In Tropic of Capricorn, Henry Miller presents a series of diverse characters, each emblematic of the chaotic and contradictory nature of human existence. His protagonists are not simply individuals, but personifications of the various contradictory impulses and desires that define the human experience. Through their multifaceted personalities, Miller explores the complexities and contradictions inherent in the human condition. One of the central characters, Ben, embodies the struggle between conformity and rebellion, as he grapples with society's norms while seeking to assert his individuality. His inner conflict serves as a mirror for the wider societal tensions present in the novel's setting.

Miller masterfully portrays the dualities of Elsie's character, juxtaposing her outward appearance of strength and resilience with her inner vulnerabilities and insecurities. This complex portrait delves into the intricacies of the human emotions and psyche, highlighting the simultaneous coexistence of strength and fragility within each individual. Furthermore, the character of Carl represents the clash between idealism and cynicism, embodying the paradoxical nature of human aspiration and disillusionment. Through these nuanced character studies, Miller not only captures the essence of the individuals themselves, but also highlights the universal conflicts and contradictions that define human nature. He skilfully weaves together these different characters, not as isolated entities, but as interconnected threads in the complex tapestry of life, highlighting the richness and diversity of the human experience. Moreover, the exploration of the protagonists' dualities serves as a profound commentary on the wider themes of personal identity, societal norms and the quest for authenticity. By delving into the inner lives of his characters and unravelling their internal conflicts, Miller invites readers to confront the complexity of their own struggles and contradictions, fostering a deeper understanding of the human experience. In essence, 'Tropic of Capricorn' presents a profound and fascinating examination of the dualities inherent in the human psyche, offering a poignant reflection on the complexities of human nature and the perpetual struggle between contradictory impulses.

Symbolism and motifs: layers of meaning

Symbolism and motifs are essential to understanding the multiple levels of meaning in Tropic of Capricorn. Throughout the novel, Henry Miller employs a rich tapestry of recurring symbols and motifs that add depth and complexity to the narrative, inviting readers to engage in a deeper exploration of the human condition and societal constructs. One of the main motifs is the use of geographical settings to reflect the inner turmoil and restlessness of the characters. Desolate landscapes, bustling urban environments and vast expanses of nature serve as metaphors for the protagonist's internal struggles, quest for freedom and search for meaning.

The recurring imagery of industrialisation, machines and work not only underlines the dehumanising effects of modernity, but also functions as a critique of capitalist society. In addition, the representation of sexual encounters and relationships as a dominant motif reflects the characters' quest for intimacy, identity and liberation. Miller skilfully weaves these themes into the fabric of the novel, creating a rich tapestry of symbols and motifs. Symbolism permeates the narrative, with objects such as clocks, mirrors and music serving as recurring motifs that underline the cyclical nature of existence, the search for self-awareness and the ephemeral passage of time.

The use of colour, particularly the contrast between light and dark, adds another layer of symbolism, representing the dichotomies of life, the battle between good and evil, and the complexities of human experience. The symbolic representations in Tropic of Capricorn transcend mere allegory, inviting readers to engage in a nuanced interpretation of the text and to uncover meanings hidden beneath the surface. Each symbol and motif is carefully designed to intersect with the thematic explorations, creating a rich tapestry of interconnected layers that invite readers to venture deeper into the heart of the novel, challenging them to contemplate the complex nuances of human existence and societal structures. In unravelling the symbolism and motifs of Tropic of Capricorn, readers are confronted with the profound complexity of the human experience, the intertwining of personal desires and societal constraints, and the perpetual search for meaning in a chaotic world.

The challenges of writing a novel: censorship and controversy

The writing of Tropic of Capricorn proved to be a tumultuous journey for Henry Miller, who faced formidable challenges related to censorship and controversy. The unabashed depiction of explicit content and controversial themes, including sexuality and existential reflections, triggered public protests and legal battles that tested the limits of creative freedom.

Prevailing societal norms and puritanical attitudes of the time cast a shadow over Miller's groundbreaking work, leading to severe censorship and outright bans in several countries. Despite advocating an authentic representation of human experience and emotion, Miller faced vehement opposition and condemnation from moral authorities and conservative factions. This burgeoning discontent sparked debates about the limits of artistic expression and moral responsibility, propelling Miller to the centre of a relentless furore.

Through the maze of censorship and controversy, Miller defied convention and remained true to his quest for an authentic story. Unfazed by virulent criticism and legal repercussions, he has defended his right to depict the raw complexities of human existence without external constraint. This unwavering commitment to artistic integrity illustrates Miller's resilient spirit and unwavering dedication to his craft.

The difficulties encountered in the making of Tropic of Capricorn highlighted the perpetual struggle between artistic freedom and societal constraints. Miller's unwavering conviction challenged the established order, sparking crucial conversations about the ethical responsibilities of artists and the censorship of literary works. Despite the obstacles encountered, his perseverance ultimately expanded the realms of creative expression and catalysed crucial changes in the public perception of artistic freedom.

The enduring legacy of Tropic of Capricorn is a testament to Miller's indomitable perseverance in the face of adversity and serves as a lasting reminder of the battle for unbridled creative expression in a restrictive world.

The role of autobiographical elements

Henry Miller's literary work often blurs the boundaries between fact and fiction, and Tropic of Capricorn is no exception. This chapter looks at the importance of autobiographical elements in the novel, exploring their role in shaping the narrative and the reader's perception of Miller's work.

Miller's frank and unapologetic description of his own experiences and emotions forms the foundation of Tropic of Capricorn. Drawing on his own tumultuous upbringing, his adventures in Paris and his subsequent struggles, the novel is an introspective journey through the author's past. By interweaving real events with creative embellishments, Miller creates a rich tapestry that not only captivates, but also challenges readers to question the boundaries of reality and imagination.

In addition, the inclusion of autobiographical elements lends the novel an undeniable sense of authenticity. Miller's raw honesty about his own life experiences gives the story a depth and sincerity that resonates deeply with readers. The intimate and often provocative nature of the autobiographical content invites readers to confront the full spectrum of human existence, with its flaws, passions and uncertainties. In doing so, Miller establishes a deep and lasting link between his own story and the universal human condition.

Beyond the personal, the incorporation of autobiographical elements allows Miller to articulate his philosophical and existential reflections with raw emotion and veracity. Through the prism of his own encounters, he tackles themes of love, freedom and social disillusionment, offering readers not only a window into his own psyche, but also a mirror reflecting the complexities of the human experience. Drawing on his personal struggles and triumphs, Miller presents a narrative that transcends mere autobiographical documentation, evolving into a timeless exploration of the depths of the human spirit.

Ultimately, the autobiographical elements of Tropic of Capricorn demonstrate the enduring power of personal narrative. They allow readers access to the inner workings of a literary iconoclast, inviting them to embark on a transformative journey that blurs the boundaries between autobiography and art. As we journey through the rich landscape of Miller's autobiographical tapestry, we are forced to confront our own truths and confrontations, forging an unbreakable bond with the author and his enduring literary legacy.

Conclusion: Legacy and influence on modern literature

The legacy of Henry Miller's literary works goes far beyond the impact of his contemporaries; his influence on modern literature is profound and lasting. By fearlessly exploring taboo subjects, using uncompromising language and relentlessly pursuing authenticity, Miller paved the way for a new era of literary expression. His unyielding commitment to depicting the raw, unfiltered nature of human existence paved the way for generations of writers who sought to break free from traditional constraints and embrace the messy, chaotic reality of life.

One of the most significant contributions of Miller's legacy is the redefinition of what constitutes acceptable subject matter in literature. By fearlessly delving into the depths of the human psyche, unabashedly depicting the complexity of relationships and confronting societal taboos head-on, Miller shattered the boundaries of censorship and paved the way for future writers to explore the full spectrum of human experience without inhibition.

Moreover, Miller's impact on the structure and form of modern literature cannot be overestimated. His experimental narrative techniques, stream-of-consciousness writing and non-linear narratives challenged conventional norms, paving the way for a more expansive and liberated approach to storytelling. Writers of all genres have been inspired by Miller's bold disregard for traditional structures, finding the freedom to create narratives that reflect the fragmented and non-linear nature of human thought and experience.

Beyond his technical and thematic influences, Miller's legacy lives on in the philosophical foundations of modern literature. His relentless quest for personal liberation, his contempt for societal conformity and his celebration of individuality resonate deeply with contemporary writers who continue to grapple with existential questions and the human condition. The themes of freedom, authenticity and the relentless quest for truth that permeate Miller's works continue to shape and inform the contemporary literary landscape, serving as an enduring source of inspiration for writers striving to capture the essence of the human experience.

In conclusion, Henry Miller's indelible mark on modern literature is characterised by a spirit of fearless rebellion, an unyielding pursuit of truth and an unquestioning embrace of the chaotic and beautiful messiness of life. His influence transcends generations, providing a timeless model for writers who seek to challenge, provoke and ultimately illuminate the complexities of the human condition through their art.

6

The Rosy Crucifixion

Myth, Memory, and Madness

Genesis of a trilogy: Context and creation

To study the genesis of Henry Miller's monumental 'The Rosy Crucifixion' trilogy, it is imperative to consider the historical and deeply personal contexts that underpinned the formation of these literary works. Born in the turbulent milieu of the early twentieth century, Miller's trilogy emerged as an innovative exploration of desire and identity in a societal setting characterised by moral restraint and political upheaval.

At its core, the trilogy is an introspective journey that reflects Miller's own experiences, bringing to life the living tapestry of his existence. In embarking on this literary saga, Miller sought to unearth the raw, unadulterated essence of human desire and to grapple with the complex interplay between one's identity and the constraints imposed by external forces. The trilogy is an intimate chronicle of his own psychological landscape and quest for individuality amidst the dominant norms of the time.

Moreover, the creation of the trilogy was profoundly influenced by the inter-war period, marked by a palpable tension between tradition and innovation, conservatism and nascent liberalism. As such, Miller's opus is a poignant testament to the liberation and evolution of modern thought and artistic expression, challenging the societal status quo and confronting entrenched taboos on sexuality, spirituality and personal autonomy. Throughout the trilogy, Miller provocatively navigates the labyrinth of human experience, offering readers an unflinching portrait of the human psyche in all its complexity and contradictions.

Moreover, the creation of the trilogy is inextricably linked to the tumultuous experiences of Miller's life as he grapples with personal triumphs and tribulations. His sojourn in bohemian Paris, his encounters with influential artistic figures and his fervent engagement with existential philosophies undeniably left an indelible mark on the creation of the trilogy. It is in the crucible of these formative experiences that Miller has forged a narrative that defies convention and embraces the many facets of human existence. In doing so, he has woven a literary tapestry that has not only transcended its temporal origins, but also resonates with timeless relevance and universal truths.

Ultimately, the genesis of The Rosy Crucifixion trilogy represents a convergence of historical upheaval, personal revelation and bold creativity. It is a testament to Miller's unyielding commitment to delving into the deepest recesses of human experience and unravelling the enigmatic threads that bind desire and identity. As we embark on our exploration of the trilogy, it is essential to look closely at the profound genesis of Miller's magnum opus and the complex web of influences that have shaped its enduring legacy.

Sexus: Exploring desire and identity

In Sexus, Henry Miller explores the complexities of desire and identity in depth, weaving a narrative that exposes the raw, unfiltered nature of human sexuality. The novel is a visceral exploration of passion, lust and desire, exposing the complex web of emotions that underlie our most primal impulses. Miller's unflinching portrayal of carnal desires challenges societal norms and conventions, inviting readers to confront their own inhibitions and confrontations. The protagonist, paralleling Miller's own experiences, embarks on a relentless quest for fulfilment, seeking not only physical gratification but also a deeper understanding of his own identity.

Through evocative prose and heartfelt introspection, 'Sexus' offers an in-depth examination of the symbiotic relationship between desire and self-discovery. The novel serves as a canvas on which Miller paints a vivid tapestry of human sensuality, capturing the peaks and valleys of erotic expression with unflinching honesty. At its core, 'Sexus' is a deeply personal exploration, peeling back the layers of societal conditioning to expose the raw authenticity of human desire.

Moreover, 'Sexus' serves as a vehicle for examining the intertwined nature of desire and existential contemplation. Miller crafts a narrative that transcends mere physical intimacy, delving into the existential implications of desire and its influence on human experience. As the protagonist navigates a world filled with sexual encounters and emotional entanglements, Miller deftly dissects the multifaceted nature of desire, explaining its importance in shaping one's sense of self and purpose.

Miller's masterful prose and profound insights elevate 'Sexus' beyond mere emotion, transforming it into a contemplative exploration of human aspiration and the search for fulfilment. Through this powerful narrative, Miller challenges readers to re-evaluate their understanding of desire and identity, urging them to embrace the complex interplay between physical, emotional and existential desires. Sexus' is a testament to Miller's ability to strip away the veneer of societal conditioning, exposing the raw, unvarnished truths that define our most intimate experiences.

Plexus: Navigating the labyrinth of the mind

Henry Miller's 'Plexus' delves into the intricacies of the human psyche, serving as a veritable atlas for navigating the enigmatic terrain of the mind. In this section, we embark on an odyssey through the labyrinthine passages of thought, emotion and consciousness that characterise Miller's bold literary exploration. Through a tapestry of introspective reflection and uncompromising self-analysis, Miller concocts an evocative portrait of the human experience, exposing the raw, unfiltered complexities that lie at the heart of existence.

At the heart of 'Plexus' is an exploration of the complex links between the realms of the conscious and the subconscious. Miller artfully untangles the interplay of desires, fears and aspirations that shape human behaviour, presenting a compelling argument for embracing the multiple contradictions of our nature, rather than seeking to expunge or repress them. As the story meanders, the reader is confronted with the stark reality of the human condition - a kaleidoscope of impulses, memories and aspirations that resist easy categorisation.

Moreover, 'Plexus' serves as a philosophical crucible in which Miller synthesises disparate aspects of the human experience, prompting readers to confront the paradoxes that define their lives. Through a series of introspective vignettes, Miller invites us to contemplate the essence of identity, the fluidity of time and the enduring power of memory. The narrative unfolds like a rich palimpsest, each layer revealing new depths of understanding and revelation. As we immerse ourselves in Miller's introspective ruminations, we are forced to reassess our own preconceptions and beliefs, confronting the spectres of doubt and uncertainty that haunt our own inner landscapes.

Ultimately, 'Plexus' challenges readers to navigate the labyrinth of their own minds, inviting them to embrace the contradictions and inherent complexities that define the human experience. It invites us to venture beyond the boundaries of conventional thought and grapple with the turbulent undercurrents that shape our perception of ourselves and the world. Through a symphony of introspection, philosophical enquiry and emotional resonance, 'Plexus' forces us to confront the multifaceted nature of our being, embarking on an intellectual and emotional expedition that transcends the boundaries of traditional narrative.

Nexus: Integrating past and present

The third part of Henry Miller's 'The Rosy Crucifixion' trilogy, Nexus delves into the complex web of influences from the past and their repercussions on the present. This section serves as a bridge between memory and immediacy, seamlessly integrating the protagonist's formative experiences with his present reality. As the story unfolds, the reader is taken on a journey of self-discovery and revelation as the protagonist grapples with the tumult of life. Exquisite prose mingles with raw emotion, drawing the reader into a world where the past is not simply a relic, but an active participant in shaping the present.
Through evocative storytelling, Miller artfully captures the essence of existence, describing the resounding impact of history on the here and now. The characters, settings and events of yesteryear resonate throughout the book, infusing the narrative with a palpable sense of continuity and interconnectedness. The author skilfully weaves a tapestry of experiences,

blurring the boundaries between what was and what is, ultimately illustrating that the past is not a fixed entity, but rather an inflexible presence in the fabric of our lives. In this vast exploration of temporal fluidity, Miller masterfully addresses the eternal struggle to reconcile one's personal history with the demands of the present moment.

By ingeniously interweaving past and present, Nexus offers profound insights into the eternal human quest for meaning and belonging. Themes of nostalgia, identity and the cyclical nature of existence are inextricably woven into the narrative, inviting readers to embark on an introspective odyssey through the corridors of time. As the protagonist confronts the ghosts of a bygone era, unresolved conflicts and long-buried desires, the reader discovers the incessant interplay between memory and immediate experience. Nexus is a testament to Miller's ability to unravel the complex intersections between past and present, prompting readers to contemplate the profound implications of their own history on their present journey. Through poignant reflections and startling revelations, Nexus inspires contemplation of man's universal effort to harmonise the timelines of our lives, affirming the timelessness and relevance of Miller's literary work.

Symbolism and archetypes in Miller's narrative

Henry Miller's literary work abounds in a rich symbolism and archetypal motifs that give his stories depth and complexity. Throughout his work, Miller skilfully uses symbols and archetypes to convey profound psychological and existential themes, inviting readers to delve deeper into the layers of meaning in his prose. One of the recurring symbols in Miller's stories is the figure of the labyrinth, which often represents the complex nature of human consciousness and the daunting journey of self-discovery. The labyrinth serves as a metaphor for the complexities of life, reflecting the twists and turns of the human psyche as characters navigate their inner landscapes.

Miller frequently uses the archetype of the wanderer or seeker, embodied in his protagonists' quests for self-realisation and personal freedom. These archetypal figures embody the universal aspiration to fulfilment and the perpetual quest for meaning in a world full of contradictions and ambiguities. In addition, the crucifixion motif appears as a powerful symbol in Miller's narrative, evoking themes of suffering, sacrifice and redemption. This symbolic motif underlines the existential trials faced by his characters and symbolises the transformative nature of their trials.

Beyond the individual symbols, Miller weaves a tapestry of archetypal characters, such as the femme fatale, the wise man and the trickster, each adding depth and nuance to the thematic tapestry of his stories. Through these symbolic elements, Miller invites readers to engage with timeless themes of human experience such as love, loss and the relentless pursuit of authenticity. By delving into the complex web of symbols and archetypes in Miller's stories, readers are led to explore the universality of these motifs, recognising their resonance in the collective unconscious and their enduring relevance to the human condition.

The interweaving of reality and fantasy: An analysis

In the captivating world of Henry Miller's 'The Rosy Crucifixion' trilogy, the boundaries between reality and fantasy are fluid and elusive. As we immerse ourselves in Miller's masterful narrative, we witness a seamless integration of the everyday and the extraordinary, blurring the boundaries between what is real and what is imagined. Through in-depth analysis, we discover how Miller uses a unique blend of realism and surrealism to paint a rich tapestry of human experience. The interweaving of reality and fantasy is a literary device that transcends traditional narrative, taking readers on a sobering journey into the depths of the human psyche. Miller's astute description of characters and events challenges conventional perceptions, inviting readers to question the very nature of truth and illusion.

This deliberate interweaving encourages readers to explore the complexities of life through a lens that combines the mundane and the miraculous. It encourages us to contemplate the interconnectedness of seemingly disparate elements, underlining the inherent enigma of existence. By seamlessly merging reality and imagination, Miller offers a profound meditation on the human condition, heralding a narrative that transcends the limits of ordinary storytelling. The blurred boundaries between reality and fantasy force readers to confront their own perception of the world, provoking introspection and philosophical questioning. As we navigate the intricate web of Miller's prose, we are led to reflect on the fluidity of truth and the enduring power of imagination. This exploration ultimately leads to a deeper understanding of the multifaceted nature of human experience, highlighting the indelible influence of reality and fantasy in shaping our worldview. The fusion of these elements results in a captivating tapestry of human emotion and reflection that resonates deeply and universally with readers.

The influence of mythic tradition

Literature often draws on the source of mythic tradition, wrapping stories in a timeless aura that resonates with universal themes and archetypal motifs. In dissecting The Rosy Crucifixion trilogy, it is impossible to ignore the profound influence of mythic tradition on Henry Miller's literary tapestry. Miller skilfully weaves a rich tapestry of mythopoetic elements, imbuing his prose with echoes of ancient tradition and the symbolism of heroic quests. His protagonist's journey reflects the archetypal odyssey of the hero, marked by trials, tribulations and encounters with symbolic figures who embody universal truths. The mythical landscape becomes a canvas on which Miller paints a visceral representation of human triumphs and tragedies, transcending the limits of linear time. Drawing on these enduring mythic currents, Miller crafts a narrative that resonates in a primal way, inviting readers to embark on an introspective expedition through the collective unconscious. Through allegorical characters and mythic allusions, he elevates his characters' personal struggles to the universal, ultimately reflecting the eternal struggle for meaning and self-discovery. This infusion of mythic tradition fosters a sense of timelessness, anchoring the story in a complex web of cultural and existential meanings. Moreover, Miller's deft assimilation of mythic motifs serves as an intellectual conduit, blending the contemporary with the primordial, inviting readers to grapple with eternal themes of identity, love and existential purpose. In this way, 'The Rosy Crucifixion' transcends its temporal framework, taking on a mythic dimension that allows it to resonate with readers of all generations and cultures. Miller's invocation of mythic tradition invites readers to engage in a process of collective remembrance and introspection, forging a profound link between the individual and the archetype. In this way, readers become participants in a timeless ritual, engaging in a spiritual and intellectual quest that transcends the confines of the printed page. In this way, The Rosy Crucifixion is not only a literary testament, but also a testament to the enduring power of mythic narratives in shaping our understanding of human experience.

Memory as metaphor: constructing history

Memory is a powerful metaphor for the construction of history in Henry Miller's The Rosy Crucifixion trilogy, as it captures the essence of human experience and its complex interaction with time. Through seminal memories and introspective narratives, Miller blurs the boundaries between personal memory and collective history, weaving a complex tapestry that challenges conventional notions of truth and perception. The trilogy becomes a means of exploring the fluidity of memory, depicting it as both a faithful chronicler and a cunning deceiver.

Miller's masterful use of memory as metaphor not only elevates the literary landscape, but also invites readers to contemplate the very nature of memory and its role in shaping individual and societal narratives. Whether delving into the depths of his own past or resurrecting bygone eras through his characters, Miller uncovers the profound links between memory and identity, showing how our memories shape our understanding of ourselves and others.

The Rosy Crucifixion' also presents memory as an active agent in the construction of history, emphasising its transformative power in the reinterpretation of the past. By interweaving personal anecdotes with historical events, Miller highlights the malleability of memory and its ability to breathe new meaning into established chronicles. This deliberate blurring of the boundaries between personal and historical memories underlines the dynamic relationship between individual experiences and the broader currents of time, offering a rich tapestry of perspectives on the human condition.

In essence, Miller's poignant exploration of memory as metaphor transcends mere nostalgia, weaving a compelling narrative that confronts the reader with the fragility and resilience of memory. By depicting memory as a shaper of history, the trilogy offers a profound reflection on the subtleties of storytelling and the elusive nature of truth. With its multi-faceted depiction of memory, 'The Rosy Crucifixion' invites readers to embark on a journey beyond the limits of linear time, inviting them to contemplate the labyrinthine corridors of human consciousness and the lasting imprints of collective memory.

Madness and insight: the artist's struggle

In the crucible of creative expression, Henry Miller grapples with the enigmatic duality of madness and insight, a recurring theme in his literary work. At the heart of his artistic endeavour, Miller confronts the tumultuous terrain of the human psyche, plunging into the depths of madness and enlightenment. His introspective exploration offers a profound insight into the complexities of the creative process and the unbridled madness that often accompanies it.

Miller's description of madness transcends the conventional notion of mental instability, for he sees it as a form of radical re-examination - a breakdown of existing structures and paradigms. His direct encounters with surreal episodes, psychological upheavals and disorientating existential crises are laid bare in the tapestry of his autobiographical narratives, inviting readers to witness the raw, unfiltered turmoil of the artist's psyche.

At the heart of this struggle is an inner quest for authenticity and free expression - an unwavering commitment to probing the unconventional corners of the human condition. As Miller struggles with the paradoxical relationship between lucidity and madness, his prose is a revealing testament to the transformative power of artistic fervour, punctuated by moments of profound clarity in the midst of chaos. This relentless quest for truth through madness underscores the artist's indomitable spirit, perpetually in search of an elusive gnosis beyond the constraints of societal norms.

The evocative intersection of madness and insight in Miller's work remains emblematic of the perpetual tension between artistic creation and the inherent psychological anguish it entails. Through a lens that is both poetic and philosophical, Miller takes an insightful look at the dichotomous nature of the human psyche, revealing the subtleties of human experience in the libidinal tableau of his prose. Her unyielding commitment to exploring the darkest recesses of the mind offers readers an unvarnished portrait of the artist's internal battles, where moments of frenzied inspiration blend seamlessly with periods of tumultuous introspection.

Ultimately, the artist's struggle is painted in chiaroscuro - the interplay of light and shadow - illuminating the labyrinthine passage to creative enlightenment. In confronting the abyss of madness, Miller uncovers indelible truths that lie dormant in the collective unconscious, paving the way for a narrative that resonates eternally in its poignant portrayal of the artist's perpetual dance between torment and transcendence.

Critical reception and lasting legacy

Henry Miller's provocative and groundbreaking literary trilogy, The Rosy Crucifixion, received a tumultuous reception on its release, as its unflinching depiction of human experience and rejection of societal norms challenged the status quo of the time. Critics were divided, some describing Miller's work as vulgar and obscene, while others hailed it as a bold and necessary reimagining of the novel form. This polarised reaction not only testifies to the controversial nature of Miller's prose, but also underlines the profound impact of his writing on the literary landscape.

Despite initial scepticism, 'The Rosy Crucifixion' has endured as a seminal work of modern literature, influencing subsequent generations of writers and thinkers. Its uncompromising approach to exploring the depths of human consciousness, identity and desire continues to resonate with readers seeking an unvarnished depiction of existence. Moreover, Miller's fearless dismantling of social convention and embrace of raw, unfiltered truth has cemented his legacy as a literary maverick whose influence extends far beyond his own time.

The enduring legacy of 'The Rosy Crucifixion' is reflected in its continued relevance to academic discourse and the ongoing dialogue around censorship, artistic freedom and the limits of expression. Scholars and critics have revisited Miller's work, recognising its contribution to the evolution of the novel and its enduring importance in challenging established literary norms.

Beyond the academic world, Miller's influence permeates popular culture, with references to his work appearing in music, film and the visual arts. His ability to tap into the primal aspects of human experience and lay bare the complexities of emotion and thought has cemented his place as a touchstone for creative expression across the media.

At a time of changing social mores and attitudes to sexuality and taboo subjects, 'The Rosy Crucifixion' remains an unshakeable testament to the power of literature to provoke, engage and, ultimately, transform the reader's understanding of the world. As the critical reception of Miller's work continues to evolve, one thing remains clear: 'The Rosy Crucifixion' remains a timeless exploration of the human condition, inviting readers to confront the beautiful and messy chaos of life.

7

Exploring Philosophies

Miller's Intellectual Foundations

Seeds of rebellion: Challenging conventional thinking

Henry Miller's intellectual journey was characterised by a categorical rejection of societal norms and traditional thought processes. Faced with a world that rigidly adhered to conservative values, Miller sought to challenge and dismantle these entrenched ideologies. He has fervently challenged the status quo, recognising it as an obstacle to authentic self-expression and self-fulfilment. This thematic rebellion against convention is a recurring motif in Miller's work, reflecting his resolute commitment to embracing authentic experience rather than conforming to imposed norms. By renouncing established paradigms, Miller has sought to cultivate a mindset that transcends the boundaries of traditional dogma.

Through his writings, he encourages his readers to embark on their own introspective journey, unfettered by preconceived notions and societal expectations. Miller's radicalism goes beyond mere subversion; it fosters an ethic of freedom and intellectual daring that challenges readers to question their deeply held beliefs. His refusal to succumb to the restrictions of dominant ideology is part of a wider existential quest for self-discovery and autonomy. Miller's seeds of rebellion germinate into a profound exploration of individualism and non-conformity, inspiring readers to defy conventional wisdom and embrace the limitless potential of independent thought. By rejecting societal constraints, Miller provokes a re-evaluation of cultural mores and invites readers to forge their own intellectual paths, unencumbered by the shackles of conformity. Ultimately, the story of defiance of orthodox thought invites readers to free themselves from the constraints of societal pressures and moral diktats, forcing them to seek authenticity and personal truth without inhibition.

The influence of Nietzsche: the birth of a radical state of mind

Friedrich Nietzsche, the enigmatic and provocative philosopher, exerted a decisive influence on Henry Miller's intellectual development. Nietzsche's writings were imbued with a rebellious spirit that defied conventional morality and challenged the established order. Miller, captivated by Nietzsche's radical ideas, found a kindred spirit in the philosopher's wholehearted embrace of individualism and rejection of traditional values. Nietzsche's concept of the 'Übermensch' or 'superman' resonated deeply with Miller, who saw in it a call to transcend societal constraints and forge one's own destiny. This rejection of societal norms and celebration of personal freedom became embedded in Miller's worldview, shaping his artistic expression and philosophical vision. Nietzsche's affirmation of the complexities, contradictions and chaos inherent in life found fertile ground in Miller's conception of existence.

The philosopher's assertion that 'God is dead' and the consequent need for humanity to create meaning and value in a seemingly meaningless world resonated throughout Miller's work, infusing it with a sense of existential urgency and purpose. Moreover, Nietzsche's critique of herd mentality and emphasis on individual creativity and self-expression allowed Miller to escape conformity and chart his own course as a writer and thinker. Delving deeper into Nietzsche's work, Miller encountered the recurring themes of amor fati (love of destiny) and eternal recurrence, concepts that profoundly influenced his perception of existence. Amor fati, with its call to embrace and affirm the totality of one's life, became a guiding principle in Miller's quest for authenticity and acceptance of life's beauty and suffering. Eternal recurrence, with its notion of the infinite repetition of existence, prompted contemplation of the cyclical nature of time and experience, fuelling Miller's introspective explorations of memory, desire and the human condition. In this way, Nietzsche's radical philosophy served as a catalyst for Miller's development of a fiercely independent spirit and a deep reverence for the vitality of existence.

Surrealist inspirations: Art beyond reality

Delving into the realm of Surrealist inspirations, we discover Miller's deep fascination with an artistic movement that sought to liberate the subconscious and challenge traditional notions of reality. Surrealism, with its dreamlike imagery, irrational juxtapositions and exploration of the unconscious, captivated Miller and significantly influenced his artistic and literary endeavours. The Surrealist movement, initiated by André Breton and Salvador Dalí, encouraged artists to delve into their deepest thoughts and desires, blurring the boundaries between dreams and reality. For Miller, surrealism was a gateway to transcend conventional boundaries, allowing him to weave a tapestry of experiences, emotions and fantasies onto the canvas of his writing. Embracing the unruly nature of the unconscious, Miller's prose resonated with the transformative power of Surrealist art, challenging readers to question their perceptions and embrace the enigmatic nature of human existence.

Surrealism became a liberating force for Miller, who saw its challenge to logic and reason as a reflection of his own rejection of societal norms and constraints. Drawing on surrealism, Miller created a literary landscape that transcended the mundane, inviting readers to explore the intricacies of the human psyche and unearth the raw, unfiltered truths hidden beneath the veneer of everyday life.

Miller was drawn to the work of artists such as René Magritte, Max Ernst and Joan Miró, whose creations evoke a sense of mystery, wonder and introspection. The interplay of symbolism, metaphor and subconscious imagery resonates with Miller's quest for authenticity and personal expression, prompting him to infuse his stories with the same ineffable allure that characterises Surrealist masterpieces. By immersing himself in the world of Surrealist inspiration, Miller has sculpted a literary cosmos where reality mingles with the ethereal, where the boundaries between waking consciousness and dreams blur into an indistinguishable continuum. In so doing, Miller invited readers to take part in a journey beyond the limits of ordinary perception, inciting them to embrace the infinite possibilities of imagination and introspection. Surrealist inspirations permeated Miller's work, imbuing his prose with a sense of otherworldly enchantment that defies rational explanation. As we navigate the exploration of Miller's Surrealist inspirations, we discover a profound reverie that transcends the limits of the tangible world, drawing us into a kaleidoscopic realm of boundless creativity and unfathomable depth.

Eastern philosophies: Embracing the Tao

Henry Miller undertook a profound exploration of Eastern philosophies, in particular the Tao.

The Tao, rooted in ancient Chinese wisdom, embodies a philosophy that emphasises living in harmony with the natural order of the universe. Miller was drawn to the mystical and enigmatic nature of the Tao, finding comfort and inspiration in its teachings. His immersion in Eastern thought provided a counterweight to the Western ideologies that prevailed in his formative years, offering him a new perspective on existence and spirituality.

By embracing the Tao, Miller adopted a more holistic and interconnected view of the world, transcending the dichotomies that often plague Western thought. He sought to integrate the dualities of life, recognising the balance and rhythm inherent in all things. Through his writings, Miller not only explored the philosophical foundations of the Tao, but also sought to embody its principles in his life experiences. The concept of Wu Wei, or effortless action, resonated deeply with Miller, shaping his approach to creativity, relationships and personal fulfilment. It encouraged him to surrender to the flow of life, to embrace spontaneity and to trust in the natural unfolding of events.

Miller's adherence to the Tao went beyond intellectual curiosity; it became a guiding principle that permeated his ethos as a writer and seeker of truth. Moreover, his interactions with Eastern thought served as a catalyst for a deeper understanding of the interconnectedness and universal flow of existence. Drawing on the timeless wisdom of Taoism, Miller found a profound source of inspiration that informed his worldview and artistic expression. By combining his exposure to Eastern philosophies with his own introspective reflections, Miller has pushed back the boundaries of his intellectual and spiritual pursuits, opening up new avenues of self-discovery and inner transformation.

Existentialism and individual freedom

Existentialism, a major philosophical movement that emerged in the twentieth century, had a profound influence on Henry Miller's intellectual foundations and literary research. At the heart of existentialist philosophy is an emphasis on individual freedom and the responsibility of each person to define his or her own existence. The rejection of traditional values and norms, coupled with a recognition of the absurdity and ambiguity of life, became fundamental elements of Miller's worldview and creative expression.

At the heart of existentialist thought is the concept of 'existence precedes essence', which asserts that individuals are not defined by predetermined roles or inherent characteristics, but forge their identity through their actions and choices. This notion freed Miller from having to conform to society's expectations and encouraged him to explore the depths of his own consciousness without predetermined constraints. Through his writing, he sought to depict the raw, unfiltered human experience, devoid of societal constructs or idealised narratives.

Furthermore, existentialism advocates the idea of an authentic life, advocating that individuals confront the anguish and uncertainty inherent in existence while embracing the freedom to find meaning in the midst of chaos. In Miller's literary works, this authenticity is palpable, as he fearlessly delves into the complexity of human emotions, relationships and desires, painting a picture of existence that transcends conventional moral judgements and societal conventions.

The philosophy of existentialism also emphasises the importance of personal responsibility and the consequences of one's choices. For Miller, this meant confronting the repercussions of his unconventional lifestyle and unabashedly tackling taboo subjects, challenging the norms of his time.

His commitment to self-expression and his relentless pursuit of artistic truth exemplify the existentialist ethos of embracing individual action and owning one's own narrative.

Furthermore, existentialism addresses the theme of anxiety, recognising the pervasive sense of unease that accompanies the realisation of one's freedom and the burden of creating meaning in a seemingly indifferent world. Miller's introspective explorations and candid reflections encapsulate the existential fear and internal conflict prevalent in the human condition, offering a poignant commentary on the complexities of navigating the modern world with integrity and purpose.

Finally, by combining existentialist principles with his literary endeavours, Miller conveyed to his audience a profound sense of autonomy and self-discovery, inviting them to engage with the eternal questions of existence and embrace the liberating power of individual freedom.

Rooted in chaos: Order as illusion

In exploring Henry Miller's intellectual foundations, the concept of chaos, intrinsic to human experience, emerges as a dominant theme. Central to Miller's paradigm of philosophical reflection is the notion that order is illusory and ultimately untenable. Adhering to the tenets of existentialism and drawing on his own reservoir of experience, Miller offers a provocative dissection of conventional understandings of order and structure. He argues that beneath the veneer of societal constructs lies an inherent chaos that defies categorisation or containment. This profound recognition serves as a rallying cry to embrace the innate disorder of existence, deconstruct the fallacious pursuit of artificial harmony and cultivate an unbridled authenticity in life.
Miller's perspective resonates with a deep belief in the transformative pow-

er of chaos, reframing it not as a force to be feared but as a source of creativity and renewal. Chaos then becomes the fertile ground from which innovation and insight emerge, evoking a sense of liberation from the constraints of imposed order. Drawing on his own experiences and observations, Miller invites readers to confront the chaos inherent in themselves and their environment, challenging them to unravel the fabrications of false stability and confront the raw, unadulterated truths that lie beneath. Through this lens, the dichotomy between order and chaos dissolves, giving way to a liberated perspective that embraces the wild, unpredictable essence of life. It is in this whirlwind of disorder that Miller finds the very essence of existence, arguing for a departure from the stifling grip of artificial equilibrium and a return to the primitive, authentic expressions of being.

The hermit and the mystic: solitude as illumination

In exploring Henry Miller's intellectual foundations, we look at the profound concept of solitude as a path to enlightenment. In embracing solitude, Miller did not simply want to escape the pressures of society, but deliberately chose to find inner truth and spiritual enlightenment. The hermit, in the traditional sense, withdraws from the earthly world to seek transcendence, often through contemplation and introspection. Similarly, the mystic seeks a deeper connection with the divine, striving to achieve unity with the universe. Miller's perspective blends these archetypes, describing solitude as the crucible of self-discovery and enlightenment. Throughout his writings, he defends the idea that authentic understanding and growth can only occur in moments of solitary reflection, away from external distractions and influences. This theme runs throughout his work, where characters embark on personal odysseys, navigating the landscapes of their own minds in search of higher truths.

For Miller, solitude is not synonymous with isolation, but rather with a sacred space in which to discover the complexities of human existence. It provides fertile ground for creativity, introspection and communion with the forces that shape our consciousness. Moreover, by embracing solitude, we can achieve a heightened awareness of the interconnectedness of all life forms, transcending the limitations of the ego and societal constructs. The symbiotic relationship between the hermit and the mystic in Miller's philosophy embodies the quest for individual authenticity and universal understanding. It encourages us to reconsider the value of moments spent in peaceful solitude, inviting us to recognise the potential for profound insights and transformative revelations. In essence, Miller's portrait of solitude as enlightenment invites readers to explore the depths of their own inner world, to seek meaning beyond the tumultuous currents of contemporary existence, and to discover the profound wisdom that comes from silent communion with oneself.

The Dissonance of Modernity: A Critique

In examining the dissonance of modernity, we are forced to confront the conflict between our innate human impulses and the constraints imposed by the contemporary world. This disjunction between our primitive inclinations and the societal structures that seek to regulate and govern them forms the core of our critique. Modernity, with its emphasis on rationalisation and efficiency, often forces individuals to adopt predefined roles and expectations, stifling their innate desires and creativity. This dissonance manifests itself in many ways, from the alienation caused by urbanisation to the dehumanising impact of industrialisation. As we navigate this terrain, it becomes clear that the rapid pace of technological progress has outstripped our capacity to assimilate and adapt, exacerbating the discord between our intrinsic aspirations and the demands of the modern age.
The pervasive influence of consumerism and materialism compounds this

discordance, leading to a sense of existential estrangement and disillusionment. Our critique looks at the tensions between traditional values and the inexorable march of progress, exposing the fractures in our social fabric and the erosion of meaningful human bonds. We question the commodification of relationships and experiences, highlighting the profound dissonance between our quest for true fulfilment and the superficial veneer of modern life. The dissonance of modernity gives rise to a disenchanted population, struggling with an existential malaise rooted in the incongruity between personal authenticity and societal conformity. It is within this dissonant landscape that our critique seeks to unravel the complexities inherent in the modern human experience, offering a piercing examination of the fissures between our deepest selves and the external forces that seek to shape and manipulate us. Through our exploration, we strive to transcend mere critique and illuminate the path to reconciliation, arguing for a holistic re-evaluation of societal paradigms and a rediscovery of the authentic human spirit amidst the cacophonous discord of modernity.

Eroticism and spiritual unification

Henry Miller's exploration of eroticism goes beyond mere physicality, delving into the realms of spiritual unification and transcendence. In his work, the intertwining of the sensual and the spiritual becomes a central theme, reflecting an attempt to reconcile the carnal desires of the body with the yearning for a deeper connection. Miller's approach to eroticism is not one of superficial indulgence, but rather one of self-discovery and metaphysical exploration. Through his writings, he challenges society's taboos and conventions, seeking to liberate the erotic experience from the shackles of moral repression.

Drawing on Eastern philosophies and mysticism, Miller explores the concept of erotic energy as a powerful force for spiritual awakening and enlightenment. He embraces the idea that the union of lovers transcends the physical act, serving as a gateway to a higher consciousness and a merging of souls. His prose exudes an almost mystical reverence for the transformative power of the erotic encounter, interweaving the corporeal and the divine in a tapestry of profound significance.

Moreover, Miller's depiction of eroticism is deeply rooted in a celebration of individual freedom and authenticity. Her characters embody a raw, unabashed sensuality that defies societal norms, embracing their desires without inhibition. This unbridled expression of passion becomes a vehicle for self-expression and liberation, echoing the broader themes of existentialism and rebellion against societal constraints.

At the heart of Miller's exploration of eroticism is the notion of the sacred - the idea that the union of bodies embodies a spiritual sanctity that transcends the limits of morality or convention. This reverence for erotic experience as a path to transcendence underlines Miller's philosophical position on the interconnectedness of the physical and the metaphysical. It is through the unification of the erotic and the spiritual that Miller presents a holistic vision of human experience, one that seeks to reconcile the complexities of desire with the yearning for transcendence. Her evocative prose invites the reader to contemplate the boundaries of the self, the eros of existence and the profound possibilities inherent in the intertwining of the physical and the spiritual.

Inner Pilgrimages: Reflections on Personal Beliefs

Inner pilgrimages, as Miller called them, were a central theme in his work, encapsulating his relentless quest for self-discovery and understanding. Rooted in a deep sense of individualism, Miller's writings are imbued with a fervent desire to unravel the complexities of existence, taking readers on a journey of philosophical revelation.

Miller's inner pilgrimages are marked by a rejection of societal norms and an unwavering commitment to seeking truth beyond conventional boundaries. His stories bear witness to the human spirit's unyielding quest for authenticity and meaning in a world beset by discord. As we navigate Miller's intellectual landscape, we discover a rich tapestry of experiences that challenge entrenched ideologies and invite us to re-evaluate our own belief systems.

Through evocative prose and thought-provoking reflections, Miller invites us to embark on an introspective odyssey, urging us to confront our deepest convictions and embrace the transformative power of self-exploration. The fusion of eroticism and spirituality is at the heart of this enterprise, as Miller contemplates the complex intersection between physical desire and the transcendent realms of consciousness. Her unflinching exploration of the human psyche forces readers to confront the dichotomies of their own spiritual and carnal inclinations, prompting them to take a deeper look at the complexities inherent in our existential fabric.

As we accompany Miller on his inner wanderings, we are confronted with the paradoxes and contradictions that define the human condition, forcing us to confront our fears, desires and aspirations. Through the prism of Miller's personal revelations, we are encouraged to embark on a path of self-discovery, embracing the nuanced interplay of identity, morality and the inexorable pursuit of ultimate truths.

Ultimately, 'Inner Pilgrimages: Reflecting on Personal Beliefs' is both an exercise in introspection and an invitation to participate in a universal journey of self-realisation. Miller's frank introspection challenges us to transcend the boundaries of dogma and tradition, encouraging readers to cross the chasm between rationality and spirituality. This chapter is a testament to the single-minded individualism and unwavering quest for truth that characterise Henry Miller's enduring literary legacy.

8

The Colossus of Maroussi

A Journey to Transcendence

The trip to Greece

Henry Miller's trip to Greece marked a transformative period in both his personal life and his literary career. Venturing to the cradle of Western civilisation, Miller discovered an ancient land steeped in mythology, art and philosophy that would inexorably shape his vision of the world and his artistic expression. The allure of Greece cast a powerful spell over Miller, triggering a deep connection that permeated his being and reverberated in his creative work. Amid the timeless ruins and verdant landscapes, he found a sanctuary that resonated with the rebellious spirit at the heart of his being.

Immersing himself in the vibrant tapestry of Greek culture, Miller delved into its rich history, absorbing the ethos of a civilisation that celebrated the human experience in all its complexity. From the rituals of the Dionysian feast to the stoic wisdom of the ancient philosophers, he discovered a multifaceted mosaic of existence that reinvigorated his perception of reality. This immersion in the palpable echoes of antiquity gave rise to a fervent passion that drove him to explore and reinterpret the essence of Greek identity through his unique lens.

The juxtaposition of past and present in Greece inspired Miller to confront the eternal themes of love, eros and the cosmic dance of life and death in a narrative style free of convention. His encounters with the warmth and spontaneity of the Greek people have infused his prose with an authenticity and vitality that reflect the fiery essence of the Mediterranean nation. Feeling the pulse of Greece coursing through his veins, Miller embarked on a quest to articulate the ineffable dimensions of the Greek spirit, transcending the boundaries of language and culture to distil its essence on the written page.

Greece became more than just a geographical location for Miller; it became a journey of self-discovery, an odyssey that freed him from the constraints of societal norms and literary conventions. Against a backdrop of olive groves and azure seas, he confronted the boundaries that define human experience, finding liberation in the convergence of raw passion and the intellectual depth characteristic of Greek thought. It was here, amidst whitewashed villages and sun-drenched cliffs, that Miller experienced a rebirth of the soul, tapping into the collective consciousness of Greece to breathe new vigour into his literary endeavours.

As we delve deeper into Miller's Greek sojourn, the captivating interaction between the author and this legendary land emerges as a monumental chapter in the annals of literary history, forever forging an indelible bond that resonates through the corridors of time.

Miller and Greece: A fatal encounter

In recounting Henry Miller's journey to Greece, it is impossible to ignore the profound impact this land had on the acclaimed author. Miller's arrival in Greece marked a decisive turning point in his life and literary career. The lure of Greece held out the promise of transcendence and liberation, offering him the chance to escape the confines of conventional society. This fateful encounter shaped his vision of existence and creativity. By immersing herself in the ancient myths and timeless landscapes of Greece, Miller found a source of inspiration that fuelled her creative endeavours. The palpable sense of history and mythology woven into the fabric of Greek culture resonates deeply with her quest for authenticity and spiritual awakening. Akin to a pilgrimage, his time in Greece became a transformative experience that imbued his writing with a profound sense of purpose and exuberance.
The dynamism of Greek life, the timeless beauty of its architecture and the wild splendour of its natural landscapes awakened something primitive in Miller, causing an awakening of his artistic sensibility. This fateful encounter engendered in Miller a fervent desire to capture the essence of Greece in his work, transcending the mere representation of a geographical place to encompass a deeper spiritual connection. Through evocative prose and introspective reflections, Miller has endeavoured to convey the enigmatic appeal of Greece and the profound impact it has had on his own inner transformation. Delving deep into the heart of Greece, its people and traditions, Miller discovered a treasure trove of experiences that enriched his understanding of the human condition and the universal yearning for spiritual fulfilment. In his encounters with the people of Greece, in particular his deep friendship with the enigmatic George Katsimbalis, Miller discovered a kindred spirit whose philosophies and joie de vivre mirrored his own. Their exchanges and camaraderie nurtured Miller's evolving perspective, infusing his writing with new depth and an unwavering respect for the resilience of the human spirit. Thus, Miller's fateful encounter with

Greece ignited a creative fire within him, propelling his literary odyssey to unparalleled heights and cementing Greece as a muse that would forever enliven his artistic legacy.

Embracing the Greek landscape

Henry Miller's arrival in Greece marked a profound shift in his worldview, as he was seduced by the captivating beauty of the Greek landscape. The rugged, sun-drenched terrain, adorned with olive groves and ancient ruins, served as a powerful muse, inspiring Miller to plunge into the depths of his own creativity and contemplation. The azure shores of the Aegean Sea beckoned, offering an infinite expanse of possibility and reflection. Each sunrise and sunset painted the horizon with a palette of colours, evoking a sense of timeless wonder and introspection.

Walking the labyrinthine streets of Athens, the city's vibrant energy blended seamlessly with its rich historical tapestry, igniting Miller's imagination and stirring the depths of his soul. The Acropolis bears witness to the enduring legacy of Greek civilisation and casts a majestic shadow over the bustling metropolis. In the midst of this juxtaposition of modernity and antiquity, Miller discovered a deep respect for the resilience and creative vitality of the Greek people.

Venturing beyond the urban landscape, Miller found himself immersed in idyllic countryside, where the land bears the imprint of centuries past. The sacred site of Delphi, nestling on the steep slopes of Mount Parnassus, exudes an ethereal aura that seems to transcend the bounds of time. Here, amid whispers of ancient wisdom and enigmatic prophecies, Miller has forged a deep connection with the spiritual essence of the land, finding solace in its enigmatic embrace.

The enchanting allure of the Cyclades inspired Miller to explore the serene islands that dot the Aegean archipelago. From the whitewashed splendour of Santorini to the rugged grandeur of Crete, each island offers a glimpse into a world steeped in myth and legend. Under the cerulean canopy of infinite skies, Miller found himself captivated by the harmonious interplay of nature and human ingenuity, a symphony that resonated with the very essence of his being.

Through the lens of the Greek landscape, Miller embarked on a transformative odyssey, seeking not only to capture the ineffable beauty that surrounded him, but also to unearth the profound truths that lay dormant in his own consciousness. His encounters with the land and its people became a poignant reflection of his own inner journey, as he immersed himself in the ineffable majesty of Greece's timeless appeal.

Classical influence: Ancient myths reimagined

The allure of ancient Greek myths has captured the imagination of countless generations, their timeless tales weaving a tapestry that continues to resonate with contemporary artists and thinkers. For Henry Miller, the exploration of classical influence in his literary odyssey became a transformative journey into the heart of myth and legend. In The Colossus of Maroussi, Miller's poignant reinterpretation of these myths testifies to their enduring power and relevance. Miller's evocative prose breathes new life into age-old tales, infusing them with a modern vitality that transcends temporal and cultural boundaries.

In the Greek landscape, Miller is enveloped by the ethereal presence of ancient ruins and mythical landscapes. Each site becomes a living embodiment of stories that have endured for millennia, and he artfully interweaves his personal experiences with archetypal narratives of gods, heroes and monsters. Delving into the enigmatic allure of the ancient world, Miller explains how a visceral connection to these myths fosters a profound sense of belonging and interconnection with the spiritual lineage of humanity. The pedestrianised streets of Athens, the sun-drenched shores of Crete and the windswept cliffs of Delphi all become stages on which the timeless drama of the myths unfolds once more.

By reimagining these classic tales, Miller illuminates the profound philosophical underpinnings that continue to reverberate in human consciousness. Peeling back the layers of time and culture, he uncovers the universal truths and existential questions that emerge from the ancient texts. The struggles of mortal heroes reflect our own human difficulties, while the whims of deities reflect the mercurial nature of fate itself. Through this lens, Miller urges readers to contemplate the enduring relevance of these myths and the wisdom they hold for navigating the twists and turns of human existence.

Miller's enterprise also highlights the dynamic interplay between past and present, as he skilfully juxtaposes ancient myths with the nuances of contemporary society. By breathing new life into these tales, he underlines the enduring relevance of their themes, offering insightful commentary on the timeless aspects of human nature. As a result, 'The Colossus of Maroussi' stands as an effervescent testament to the enduring legacy of classical influence, enriching our understanding of mythology's indelible imprint on the human psyche and highlighting its ability to transcend the passage of time.

A philosophical shift: from existentialism to spirituality

Henry Miller's stay in Greece marked a profound philosophical shift in his vision of the world. Moving away from the existentialist ethic that permeated much of his earlier work, Miller transformed himself into a more spiritual understanding of existence. His immersion in ancient Greece, with its rich tapestry of myth and folklore, led him to reassess his place in the cosmos and to contemplate the interconnectedness of all forms of life.

The rugged landscape of Greece, dotted with ancient ruins and steeped in history, served as a catalyst for Miller to move away from the purely existential concerns of the self. Instead, he found himself drawn to the timeless wisdom contained in Greek mythology and the innate spirituality woven into the fabric of everyday life. This transition was not a rejection of existentialism, but rather a transcendence, a realisation that human experience encompasses both existential and spiritual dimensions.

Miller's encounters with the local people and their customs and traditions opened a window onto a world where the sacred and the profane are effortlessly intertwined. The rituals, festivals and superstitions of the Greek people became an integral part of his daily existence, prompting him to re-examine his own cultural roots and open himself up to spiritual interpretations of the mysteries of life.

The embrace of spirituality did not entail a retreat from the complexities of existence, but rather an expansion of its philosophical palate. Miller navigated this new terrain with a mixture of reverence for the ancient wisdom he encountered and a critical eye sharpened by years of wrestling with existential dilemmas. He sought to reconcile the immediacy of individual experience with the enduring truths contained in the myths and legends of antiquity.

In essence, Miller's philosophical journey to Greece brought the existential and the spiritual into harmony, testifying to the multifaceted nature of human consciousness and the eternal quest for meaning. This transformation would indelibly influence his later writings, giving them a depth and resonance that transcend the limits of mere existential introspection.

Involvement in local culture and tradition

In the heart of the Mediterranean, Henry Miller embraced the rich tapestry of Greek culture and tradition during his stay in the land of myth and legend. Immersing himself in local customs and practices, Miller found himself captivated by the timeless rituals and celebrations deeply rooted in Greek history. From vibrant festivals in honour of the ancient gods to intimate gatherings in picturesque villages, Miller sought to understand the essence of Greek identity through its people and age-old traditions.

The warmth and hospitality of the Greek community gave Mr Miller a deep sense of belonging, transcending the boundaries of language and nationality. Through shared meals and lively conversations, he immersed himself in the soul of Greece, absorbing the values and beliefs that permeate every aspect of daily life. Respect for family, respect for nature and respect for the divine permeated every interaction, shaping Miller's perception of a culture imbued with wisdom and resilience.

Wandering the labyrinthine streets and paths, Miller met artisans, storytellers and musicians preserving the art of their ancestors. He marvelled at the intricate tapestries woven by skilled hands, listened to the haunting melodies of traditional instruments and savoured the flavours of authentic cuisine bearing the imprint of centuries-old recipes. Each gathering deepened its appreciation of the interconnectedness of art, spirituality and community, highlighting the profound role of cultural expression in shaping the human experience.

Participating in local festivities, such as exuberant dances and processions, allowed Miller to bear witness to the unbroken continuity of tradition and its relevance in a rapidly changing world. The rhythm of dance and the lyrical poetry of folklore have become a living testimony to the collective memory of a people, preserving stories that span time and civilisation. Through this immersive engagement, Miller recognised universal truths embedded in the particularities of Greek culture, discovering parallels with his own quest for authenticity and transcendence.

Ultimately, Miller's intimate engagement with Greek culture and tradition served as an incandescent lens through which he contemplated the universality of the human experience. Sharing moments of laughter, contemplation and camaraderie with the locals, he realised that the essence of humanity resonated through the expressions of diverse cultures. His encounters with the richness of Greek heritage became a poignant reminder of the deep bonds that unite people across time and space, transcending language barriers and ideological divides.

Nature and art: an expression of freedom

Immersed in the idyllic setting of Greece, Henry Miller found solace and inspiration in the harmonious coalescence of nature and art. The Mediterranean landscapes served as a profound muse, inviting Miller to explore the complex link between the external environment and artistic creation. In the embrace of the Greek countryside, he experienced an unparalleled sense of freedom, liberated from societal constraints and immersed in the raw beauty of the natural world.

The craggy cliffs, azure seas and sun-drenched olive groves became his sanctuary, offering him respite from the confines of modern urbanity. It was here, amidst the timeless appeal of Greek civilisation, that Miller discovered a profound kinship with the elemental forces of earth, water and sky. The rhythmic cadence of the sea, the golden hues of the Mediterranean sunset and the ancient whispers of the olive trees converge to form a rich tapestry of sensory immersion.

Through her writing and artistic endeavours, Miller has sought to capture the ineffable essence of this pristine environment, channelling its transformative energy into evocative prose and vivid imagery. Her encounters with local craftsmen, musicians and artisans have enriched her creative experience, fostering a deep appreciation of the indigenous traditions and folk art that flourish under the Hellenic sun.

In the field of art, Miller's exploration has extended beyond the written word, embracing the visual and aural expressions of cultural heritage. From the vibrant brushstrokes of contemporary painters to the stirring melodies of traditional Greek music, he has revelled in the diverse manifestations of human creativity. His involvement with local artists testifies to the pervasive spirit of freedom that permeates Greek aesthetics, transcending linguistic barriers and ideological divides.

For Miller, the synthesis of nature and art has become an emblem of personal liberation, a testament to the transformative power of creative expression. Through his immersive encounters with the Greek landscape and its artistic milieu, he discovered a profound affirmation of the intrinsic beauty of life and the enduring resonance of human ingenuity. In the melting pot of nature and art, Miller found not only an expression of freedom, but also a poignant reminder of the interconnectedness of all creative endeavours, resonating across temporal and cultural boundaries.

Reflection and transformation

In the tranquil embrace of the Greek landscape, Henry Miller found himself immersed in a profound introspection that led to a period of reflection and transformation. Far from the hectic metropolises of Paris and New York, the idyllic setting of Greece allowed Miller to disconnect from the noise of contemporary society and plunge into the depths of himself. The serene beauty of the natural surroundings provided an ideal environment for contemplation and self-exploration.

During this introspective journey, Miller was confronted with existential questions and sought to distil the essence of human existence. His encounters with local culture and traditions prompted him to re-evaluate his own beliefs, serving as a catalyst for personal development and philosophical evolution. By engaging with the vibrant fabric of Greek life, Miller began to perceive the interconnectedness of all aspects of existence, delving into the complexities of time, mortality and human experience.

The transformative power of the Greek odyssey is strikingly reflected in Miller's writing, as she navigates the depths of her own psyche, confronting her fears, desires and spiritual aspirations. Through introspective prose and lyrical reflections, he conveys the nuances of his inner metamorphosis, inviting readers to reflect on universal truths and embrace the enigmatic journey of self-discovery.

Seeking to transcend the limits of everyday realities, Miller embarks on an exploration of the metaphysical dimensions of life, searching for meaning beyond material pursuits and societal conventions. The fusion of nature, art and spirituality became intrinsic to his quest, as he contemplated the interconnectedness of humanity and the universe. This phase of introspection marked a turning point in Miller's philosophical vision, propelling him towards a deeper understanding of the human condition and the inherent search for transcendence.

Through the prism of reflection and transformation, Miller invites readers to accompany him on a profound odyssey of the soul, navigating the limitless realms of consciousness and grappling with the ineffable mysteries of existence. The amalgam of personal experiences and metaphysical reflections intertwine to form a tapestry of introspection, resonating with the universal quest for enlightenment and the evolution of individual perception.

Transcending the ordinary: The search for meaning

At the heart of Henry Miller's exploration in 'The Colossus of Maroussi' is an unwavering quest to transcend the limitations of everyday existence and discover profound meaning amidst the tumult of life. Miller's experiences in Greece serve as the crucible for this existential journey, allowing him to plunge to the heart of human existence and search for the elusive essence of being. In his quest, he immerses himself in the rich tapestry of Greek culture, tradition and mythology, drawing inspiration from the ancient wisdom that permeates the country. Through his encounters with the Greek people, Miller discovers ideas that challenge conventional perceptions and open up pathways to enlightenment. The landscapes of Greece are not just a backdrop, but a canvas on which Miller paints his philosophical investigations, giving the natural world a deeper meaning. As he traverses the countryside and contemplates the serene beauty of the Mediterranean, he grapples with fundamental questions about the nature of reality, the human condition and the interconnectedness of all things. At the heart of this odyssey is a profound desire to transcend the ordinary and embrace a heightened awareness of the mysteries inherent in life.

For Miller, the quest for meaning becomes a pilgrimage that brings him face to face with his own limitations and preconceptions, ultimately unveiling a transcendent vision of existence that defies traditional boundaries. Through the prism of 'The Colossus of Maroussi', readers are invited to take part in this transformative odyssey, embarking on a spiritual expedition alongside Miller as he discovers timeless truths that speak to the very essence of what it means to be human.

9

Beyond Scandal:

Censorship and Literary Freedom

Scandal and censorship

From the publication of 'Tropic of Cancer' to 'Tropic of Capricorn' and 'The Rosy Crucifixion' trilogy, Miller's uncompromising exploration of sexuality, vivid language and raw depiction of human experience often provoked passionate reactions from audiences and critics alike. Adopting a frank and uninhibited narrative style, Miller fearlessly delved into taboo subjects that challenged societal norms and upset established sensibilities. As a result, his works sparked fervent debate, sparking an ongoing dialogue about censorship, artistic freedom and the role of literature in society.

The seismic impact of Miller's writings was felt far beyond the realm of literature, permeating cultural, legal and moral landscapes. Critics have grappled with the explicit nature of his prose, while admirers have revered his bold authenticity and rejection of conventional narrative paradigms. Miller's unwavering commitment to uncovering the subtleties of human existence elicited both accolades and admonitions, placing him at the heart of a fervent discourse that continues to resonate across generations. The intersection between Miller's literary legacy and the spheres of morality, decency and freedom of expression has propelled his work to the centre of profound discussions about the rights and responsibilities of authors, publishers and readers.

Moreover, while controversy surrounded his writings, the worldwide reception of Miller's work illustrated the diversity of attitudes towards artistic expression and the challenges faced by those who navigate the boundaries of society. This complex tapestry of reaction and rebuttal testifies to the enduring power of Miller's literary provocations and the complexities surrounding the implications of artistic freedom in a world bound by moral codes and censorship laws.

The birth of controversy: Miller's provocative themes

Henry Miller's literary career was marked by an uncompromising exploration of taboo subjects that challenged the moral and social conventions of his time. In groundbreaking works such as Tropic of Cancer and Tropic of Capricorn, Miller fearlessly tackled themes of sexuality, existentialism and the human condition with unprecedented frankness and crudity.

His unvarnished depiction of human desires, including explicit sexual encounters and unabashed expression of individual freedom, provoked fierce controversy and censorship. His refusal to adhere to societal norms and his relentless quest for authenticity made him a daring provocateur in the literary world.

At the heart of Miller's controversial themes is a fervent rejection of traditional values and a fervent embrace of unbridled self-expression. By openly addressing taboo subjects such as sexuality, identity and disillusionment,

Miller pushed the boundaries of acceptable discourse, forcing readers to confront uncomfortable truths about the human experience.

The unfettered depiction of sexuality in Miller's writing, often labelled vulgar and offensive in his day, served as a powerful catalyst for both condemnation and admiration. His bold depiction of erotic experiences and personal liberation clashed head-on with prevailing prudish sensibilities, setting off a storm of debate in literary circles and society at large.

Moreover, Miller's provocative themes went beyond mere shock value; they served as a lens through which he examined the complexities of human existence. By exposing the raw, unvarnished reality of life, Miller invited his audience to enter a realm of unfiltered emotion and uninhibited introspection. His unvarnished portrait of the human psyche resonated with readers seeking authentic representations of the human experience, affirming his status as a literary trailblazer.

By assuming the role of literary renegade, Miller confronted society's taboos and censorship head-on, asserting the writer's right to freedom of expression. Despite fierce opposition and endless legal battles, Miller remained steadfast in his commitment to defending artistic freedom, leaving an indelible mark on the history of literature and paving the way for future generations of writers to challenge the boundaries of acceptability.

Early reception: A shock wave in literary circles

Henry Miller's literary works often sparked controversy and provoked major reactions in literary circles. The publication of works such as Tropic of Cancer challenged prevailing societal norms and conventions, unsettling the sensibilities of many readers and critics. Miller's uncompromising exploration of taboo subjects ranging from sexuality and existentialism to the human condition and societal structures led to radical changes in the way literature was received. Literary circles were unprepared for Miller's raw, unfiltered depiction of life, which sent shockwaves through the established artistic and intellectual communities.

Critics and writers were divided by Miller's bold thematic explorations, some praising his innovative approach while others vehemently criticised his work as obscene and morally repugnant. This dichotomy has heightened the fervour surrounding Miller's writing, placing him at the centre of heated debate and discussion within the literary sphere. As visceral reactions engulfed the literary community, Miller's reputation as a provocateur and trailblazer was firmly established, cementing his position as an emblem of a controversial but pioneering literature.

The impact of Miller's early reception transcended mere literary discourse, permeating wider socio-cultural discussions. His unflinching portrayal of human experience and societal constraints challenged readers to confront uncomfortable truths and question established paradigms. In doing so, Miller triggered a transformation in attitudes and expectations about what literature could and should address, leading to a reassessment of the limits and potential of literary expression. As a result, his works generated not only controversy, but also a revitalisation of the artistic landscape, fostering a new spirit of free and unconstrained creative expression.

Ultimately, early receptions of Miller's work catalyzed a seismic shift in literary circles, serving as a catalyst for transformative dialogue and introspection. The shockwaves emanating from Miller's early forays into uncharted literary territory reverberated far beyond the confines of traditional criticism, leaving an indelible mark on the trajectory of literature and cultural discourse. It is in this tumultuous context that Miller's work has emerged as a beacon of challenge and inspiration, challenging the status quo and perpetuating an enduring legacy of creative innovation.

Legal battles: Trials and tribulations

Henry Miller's literary works often found themselves at the centre of legal battles, confronting societal norms and challenging the limits of freedom of expression. The trials and tribulations Miller faced in defending his revolutionary writings provide a fascinating account of the artistic struggle against censorship and repression. Throughout his career, Miller faced numerous legal challenges that tested the limits of freedom of expression and artistic creation. These battles not only shaped his personal life, but also left an indelible mark on the landscape of modern literature.

One of the most famous cases is that of the publication of Tropique du cancer, which encountered major legal obstacles due to its explicit content and its perception of obscenity. The legal battles surrounding the novel led Miller to confront the authorities directly, resulting in lengthy court proceedings and heated public debates. Despite this fierce opposition, Miller remained firmly convinced of the power of unbridled creative expression. His unwavering commitment to artistic freedom inspired a generation of writers and intellectuals to defy conventional mores and embrace the avant-garde. Miller's legal troubles illustrate the continuing conflict between artistic freedom and prevailing societal attitudes.

The trials and tribulations he faced reverberate through time, a stark reminder of the sacrifices made in the pursuit of unfettered artistic expression. These battles not only highlighted the contentious nature of censorship, but also provoked profound philosophical reflections on the role of the artist in a restrictive society. Miller's legal confrontations testify to his unwavering dedication to the principles of unrestricted creativity, inspiring future generations to champion the cause of intellectual freedom. Moreover, these legal battles became emblematic of the broader social and cultural changes that occurred during Miller's lifetime, marking a pivotal moment in the ongoing struggle for artistic autonomy and free self-expression. The legacy of Miller's legal battles endures as a symbol of defiance against oppressive regulations and serves as a rallying cry for artists to challenge the status quo and push the boundaries of artistic innovation.

Censorship laws: An overview of restrictions

Censorship laws have played an important role in shaping the literary landscape, often serving as a double-edged sword in the quest for artistic freedom. At different times and in different regions, governments, religious authorities and societal norms have sought to impose restrictions on writing deemed controversial or morally reprehensible. These restrictions range from outright bans and book burnings to more subtle forms of suppression, such as subtle intimidation and self-censorship.

Throughout history, censorship has been used with varying degrees of rigour, reflecting the prevailing cultural and political climates of different societies. In some cases, censorship laws have been used to maintain social order and traditional values. Conversely, they have also been used as instruments of oppression, stifling dissent and perpetuating power imbalances.

The evolution of censorship laws is closely linked to broader movements in intellectual and social history. During periods of political upheaval or moral reform, such as the Enlightenment, the Victorian era and the Cold War, censorship laws underwent substantial transformations as authorities sought to impose ideological conformity and suppress subversive thought. In the context of literature, this led to the censorship of works that challenged conventional thinking, explored taboo subjects or criticised established institutions.

Beyond explicit legal statutes, censorship can manifest itself through informal channels, including industry pressure, public condemnation and manipulation of distribution channels. These mechanisms often exert de facto censorship by influencing the content that reaches the public sphere. In publishing, editorial decisions can be strongly influenced by the perceived sensitivities of target audiences, which can lead to the pre-emptive exclusion of contentious content.

The current debate on the legitimacy of censorship has generated fervent discourse among academics, writers and activists. Proponents of censorship argue that it protects the morals of society and shields vulnerable groups from harmful influences. Opponents, on the other hand, argue that censorship undermines individual freedoms, stifles creativity and impedes intellectual progress.

As the literary world confronts the challenges of censorship, it is essential to examine the interconnected dynamics of legislation, cultural sensitivities and ethical considerations. By critically assessing the historical contexts and implications of censorship laws, we can better understand the complexity of balancing freedom of expression with community responsibilities.

Global perspectives: Reactions beyond borders

By examining the reception of Henry Miller's works beyond national borders, it becomes clear that the controversy and censorship surrounding his writings have transcended mere local scrutiny. Miller's unflinching depiction of human experience, often in brutally honest or explicitly sensual terms, elicited varied responses from diverse cultures and communities around the world. From continent to continent, his boundary-pushing stories have sparked lively debates about the boundaries of artistic expression and the role of literature in society.

In Europe, and particularly in France, where Miller lived for a long period, his bold prose found a more receptive audience than in his native America. Avant-garde literary circles in Paris embraced Miller as a fearless voice challenging conventional norms. By contrast, in the conservative societies of the time, such as Britain, Miller's writings met with severe opposition and condemnation for challenging established moral codes and social propriety.

Moving eastwards, Asia also found itself grappling with Miller's confrontational style. In Japan, Miller's raw, unabashed depiction of human desires and existential crises resonated deeply with a generation eager to break free from traditional constraints. Conversely, in more conservative regions, his work was greeted with scepticism and apprehension, seen as an affront to cultural sensibilities.

Throughout Latin America, Miller's influence can be seen in the counter-cultural movements that have emerged in response to political repression and societal constraints. His themes of liberation and individualism struck a chord with artists and intellectuals who opposed authoritarian regimes, adding a socio-political dimension to his literary impact.

The worldwide reactions to Miller's work provide an insight into the universal complexities of artistic censorship and the dynamic interplay between cultural values and creative expression. The divergent reactions are a poignant reminder of literature's enduring power to provoke, challenge and enlighten, transcending geographical boundaries to generate conversations that resonate across the tapestry of human experience.

The role of publishers and defenders

The support and advocacy of publishers played an essential role in the dissemination of Henry Miller's work, despite the vehement challenges posed by censorship and obscenity laws. Despite legal and social opposition, some courageous publishers recognised the literary value and cultural importance of Miller's writings, leading them to champion his cause. These publishers have shown an unwavering dedication to defending freedom of expression and challenging the status quo, firmly believing in the fundamental right of authors to express their ideas without undue restriction.

By adopting Miller's work, these publishers have demonstrated their commitment to promoting intellectual diversity and pushing the boundaries of artistic expression. Even in the face of legal threats and public scrutiny, they have resolutely supported Miller, positioning themselves as catalysts for social change. Their actions underline the essential role that publishers play in safeguarding the principles of freedom of expression and creating an environment where creative voices can flourish unhindered.

In addition to publishers, literary critics, academics and civil rights activists have also emerged as staunch defenders of Miller's unfettered literary expression. They rigorously defended his right to convey his thoughts and experiences authentically, placing his work in the wider context of artistic innovation and social commentary. Through passionate rhetoric and persuasive argument, they sought to dismantle the barriers imposed by the forces of censorship, striving to elevate Miller's work to its rightful place as a major contribution to modern literature.

Moreover, the collaboration between publishers and advocates served to galvanise a wider movement of artistic liberation, inspiring a burgeoning community of readers, intellectuals and creators to rally behind Miller's vision. Together, they engaged in constructive dialogues and public forums, highlighting the enduring importance of unrestricted artistic expression and the intrinsic value of dissenting voices in shaping the cultural tapestry. Their unified efforts gave impetus to the discourse on censorship, sparking meaningful conversations about the delicate balance between artistic freedom and societal responsibility.

Ultimately, the combined influence of these steadfast editors and passionate advocates helped not only to vindicate Miller's literary efforts, but also to redefine society's attitude toward creative autonomy more broadly. Their unwavering support embodied the triumph of principle over prejudice, triggering a transformative paradigm shift that reverberated across the literary landscape, ensuring that future generations would inherit a broader and more inclusive realm of artistic freedom.

Breaking barriers: obscenity trials

In the literary landscape of the twentieth century, Henry Miller was a provocative figure who challenged social norms and pushed the boundaries of artistic expression. In doing so, he faced fierce resistance from the authorities who sought to suppress his work through obscenity trials that tested the limits of freedom of expression and artistic freedom. The obscenity trials that surrounded Miller's novels, in particular 'Tropic of Cancer' and 'Tropic of Capricorn', were decisive moments in the fight for creative freedom. These trials not only highlighted the contentious nature of censorship laws, but also sparked crucial debates about the intersection of literature, morality and legal constraints.
One of the most important court cases took place in the United States, where Miller's graphic and uncompromising depiction of sexuality and existential reflections clashed with deeply held conservative values. The ensuing legal battles highlighted the conflict between an artist's right to unrestricted expression and prevailing societal norms, leading to heated

debates over whether provocative writings could be deemed obscene or had intrinsic literary value. The results of the trials had repercussions far beyond the realm of literature, profoundly influencing wider discussions about freedom of expression, individual liberties and the role of government in regulating artistic content.

These trials resulted in a spirited defence of Miller's work by lawyers, intellectuals and writers who embraced the fundamental principles of creative autonomy and the unfettered dissemination of diverse perspectives. Their impassioned plea transcended Miller's specific case and evolved into a broader movement advocating the protection of artistic expression from arbitrary censorship and moral policing. When the dust settled from these legal clashes, the legacy of the trials reverberated throughout the literary world, leaving an indelible mark on the ongoing struggle for freedom of expression and unfettered creativity. Ultimately, the landmark obscenity trials led to a profound reassessment of the relationship between literature, society and the law, changing perceptions of what constitutes artistic licence and encouraging future generations of writers to defy conventional norms in pursuit of unfettered personal expression.

Literary freedom and moral constraints

In literature, the tension between artistic freedom and societal values has always been a source of debate. Henry Miller's work, in particular 'Tropic of Cancer' and 'Tropic of Capricorn', has given rise to controversial discussions centred on the conflict between literary expression and moral standards. Defenders of literary freedom argue that artists should be allowed to explore the full spectrum of human experience, including its darkest and most controversial aspects, without restriction. They argue that this unrestricted creative freedom is essential to authentic artistic expression and the exploration of profound truths about the human condition. On the other hand, proponents of moral restraint argue that some content can be harmful or offensive to society as a whole, and argue in favour of limiting content deemed morally reprehensible. They argue that literature should respect ethical standards and not promote ideas or behaviour that are contrary to the norms and values of society.

This dichotomy raises crucial questions about the responsibilities of writers, the rights of readers and the role of censorship in a democratic society. Are there inherent limits to artistic expression? Should literature hold up a mirror to society, reflecting its complexities and contradictions, or be an agent of change that challenges dominant beliefs and conventions? As such, the controversy surrounding Miller's writings reflects wider philosophical debates about the limits of artistic freedom and the ethical considerations inherent in the production and consumption of literature. In examining this complex interplay, we are forced to confront profound questions about the intersections of artistic creativity, social responsibility and cultural evolution. These deliberations go far beyond the figure of Henry Miller himself, for they have enduring relevance in contemporary discourse and highlight the enduring conflicts inherent in the pursuit of literary truth and integrity.

The Legacy of Emancipation: The Way Forward for Writers

Reflecting on the enduring legacy of literary emancipation, it becomes increasingly clear that Henry Miller's struggles against censorship and moral constraints paved the way for future generations of writers to embrace freedom of expression. Miller's unwavering commitment to artistic autonomy and unfiltered storytelling highlighted the importance of challenging societal norms and bureaucratic constraints on creativity. Her unwavering determination in the face of opposition is a source of inspiration to contemporary and aspiring writers, encouraging them to confront taboos and push the boundaries of conventional literary discourse.

The way forward for writers is to harness the invaluable lessons learned from Miller's tumultuous journey, where resilience and perseverance triumphed over repression and denunciation. With the backdrop of Miller's trials and tribulations serving as a poignant reminder of the ongoing struggle for unfettered artistic expression, the next generation of writers has a mission to keep the torch of literary freedom burning. Echoing the essence of Miller's challenge, writers must fearlessly challenge the status quo and confront the inconvenient truths that fuel their creative endeavours. In doing so, they not only honour the sacrifices of pioneers such as Miller, but also contribute to the evolution of literature as a vehicle for profound introspection and societal change.

Moreover, to move forward, writers must take advantage of the global interconnectedness facilitated by modern technologies, enabling them to forge alliances and support networks that transcend geographical and ideological barriers. This collaborative spirit fosters an environment where diverse voices can flourish and amplify the impact of their stories, echoing Miller's vision of literary emancipation reverberating across cultural landscapes. As the literary world continues to grapple with shifting sensibilities and political climates, the way forward requires an unwavering commitment to the principles of unrestricted artistic expression. By actively engaging in the defence of intellectual freedoms, writers can consolidate the foundations laid by pioneers like Miller and preserve a future where creative expression flourishes without external constraints. Despite the continuing difficulties, the road ahead offers writers endless opportunities to redefine the boundaries of literary freedom, shaping a vibrant literary landscape that celebrates boldness, authenticity and diversity of thought.

10

Influences and Inspirations
Nietzsche to Surrealism

Nietzschean thought: The Übermensch and beyond

Friedrich Nietzsche's concept of the Übermensch, or 'superman', is a central pillar of his existential philosophy, with profound implications for the literary landscape. Originating in his seminal work Thus Spoke Zarathustra, the Übermensch embodies the pinnacle of human potential, transcending conventional moral and societal values to embrace individuality and self-realisation. In literature, this concept has inspired characters and stories that grapple with the complexities of human existence, confronting the traditional norms and ideologies that prevail in society. In exploring the idea of the Übermensch, authors have explored the struggle for authenticity, the search for personal truths and the quest for meaning amidst the chaos of existence. The concept of the Übermensch provokes introspection and philosophical questioning, challenging readers to reconsider their assumptions about morality, purpose and human potential.

Through the prism of the Übermensch, literature becomes a platform for examining the tensions between conformity and individuality, inviting readers to confront existential dilemmas and contemplate the nature of their own identity. This Nietzschean ideal not only influenced the protagonists of literature, it also served as a catalyst for pushing the boundaries of literary expression, allowing writers to challenge convention and explore unconventional narrative structures. Moreover, the Übermensch provided a framework for artistic rebellion, encouraging writers to transgress established norms and create narratives that celebrated the multifaceted nature of human experience. In this way, Nietzsche's philosophy of the Übermensch continues to resonate in the realm of literature, serving as both intellectual provocation and creative inspiration for those seeking to convey the complexities of the human condition.

The Surrealist connection: Liberating the subconscious

Surrealism, an avant-garde movement that captured the essence of dreams, desires and the unconscious, profoundly influenced the literary landscape during the 20th century. Emerging in the aftermath of the First World War, Surrealism sought to challenge rationalism and embrace the irrational, unearthing hidden truths and tapping into the deepest recesses of human consciousness. Led by the charismatic figure of André Breton, the Surrealists championed automatic writing, chance encounters and the juxtaposition of seemingly unrelated elements to provoke a sense of wonder and perplexity. The movement advocated creative liberation, urging writers to break free from conventional constraints and explore the limitless realms of the imagination.

Surrealist literature often employs the absurd and the strange, blurring the boundaries between reality and fantasy to elicit powerful emotional responses and reveal latent psychological tensions. Artists such as Salvador Dalí, René Magritte and Max Ernst transposed these principles onto canvas, creating visually arresting works that mirror the surrealist narratives of their literary counterparts. Authors such as Paul Éluard, Louis Aragon and Philippe Soupault used automatic writing techniques to bypass conscious thought and delve directly into the subconscious, giving rise to raw, unfiltered expressions of human experience. As Henry Miller navigated his own artistic journey, the surrealist ethos left an indelible mark on his work, emphasising the irrational, the dreamlike and the radical re-imagining of reality. His prose reflects the Surrealist fascination with the subconscious, as he delves into the unexplored depths of the human psyche, defying traditional narrative structures and embracing the fluidity of thought. The surrealist connection not only broadened the horizons of literature, it also revolutionised the way we perceive and interpret the world around us, inviting readers to venture into the enigmatic realm where dreams and reality intertwine.

Existential currents: grappling with the absurd

Existential currents: Grappling with Absurdity When we look at the profound influences and inspirations that shaped Henry Miller's worldview and literary discourse, the existential currents of grappling with absurdity become evident. An adherent of the existentialist philosophy propagated by such luminaries as Albert Camus and Jean-Paul Sartre, Miller confronted the absurdity inherent in the human condition with unwavering introspection and intellectual fervour. The heart of this philosophical exploration lies in the paradoxical nature of existence, confronted by the insignificance of human life against the backdrop of an indifferent universe. This profound contemplation of the meaninglessness of life amplified Miller's literary investigations, imbuing his work with a raw, unfiltered depiction of human struggle.

Miller's theme of the absurd manifests itself in his characters' relentless search for individual purpose and meaning in an inherently chaotic and arbitrary world. At the heart of his narrative tapestry is a poignant depiction of human struggle, juxtaposing hope with despair, resilience with futility. Moreover, his existential canvas transcended the bounds of traditional literary conventions, transcending conventional narrative to reflect the existential dilemmas inherent in the human psyche. Through introspective protagonists navigating the labyrinth of existence, Miller highlighted the perpetual tension between despair and transcendence, inviting readers to confront their own existential dilemmas.

Delving deeper, Miller's struggle with absurdity resonates with the fundamental tenets of existentialism - a powerful affirmation of individual agency and responsibility coalesced with a recognition of the chaos and ambiguity inherent in life. In this exploration, the role of consciousness as both gift and burden emerges distinctly, depicting the irrevocable loneliness of human existence juxtaposed with an innate yearning for interconnectedness. This evocation of visceral emotional landscapes interspersed with intellectual dissonance defines Miller's unparalleled approach to grappling with absurdity - an unwavering reflection on the human condition at its most vulnerable and resilient. Thus, in the context of Miller's work, the exploration of existential currents becomes a pulsating current that reverberates through his profound narratives, encapsulating the very essence of human existence in its nuanced and enigmatic folds.

The Eastern perspective: Zen and the art of detachment

In exploring Henry Miller's influences and inspirations, we cannot overlook the profound impact of the Eastern perspective on his literary and philosophical vision. The Zen concept of detachment, rooted in the teachings of Buddhism, captivated Miller and seeped into the fabric of his worldview. The essence of detachment, as championed in Zen philosophy, goes beyond simple disengagement; it encompasses a profound state of non-attachment, allowing individuals to embrace the impermanence of existence without succumbing to emotional entanglement. Miller found resonance in this approach and incorporated it into his narrative explorations with a masterly touch.

The art of detachment, revealed through the Zen lens, permeates Miller's work, infusing his prose with a sense of serene observation and acceptance. Through his writing, readers meet characters who navigate the tumultuous currents of life with an underlying sense of detachment, achieving a state of graceful balance in the midst of chaos. This encapsulation of Zen principles in literary expression demonstrates Miller's ability to channel Eastern philosophies into Western literature, enriching the tapestry of his narrative art.

Furthermore, the influence of Zen permeates Miller's depiction of nature, infusing his descriptions with an almost palpable sense of interconnectedness and harmony. The seamless integration of human experience with the natural world reflects the Zen principle of unity and interdependence. With meticulous attention to detail, Miller demonstrates a deep respect for the ephemeral beauty of existence, reflecting the contemplative aesthetic intrinsic to Zen thought.

Moreover, the notion of 'satori' - often described as a sudden moment of awakening or enlightenment - finds its parallel in Miller's description of the revelatory experiences that punctuate her characters' journeys. These instances of profound insight and self-realisation echo the Zen quest to transcend the constraints of ordinary perception in order to achieve profound clarity and understanding. Miller skilfully interweaves these threads, weaving a narrative that subtly draws on the mysticism of Zen teachings without overtly imitating them, giving his work an enigmatic depth.

By incorporating the Eastern perspective, in particular the Zen philosophy of detachment and interconnection, Miller broadens the scope of his literary work, presenting readers with a world that resonates with timeless wisdom and a contemplative allure. This seminal influence underscores the multifaceted nature of Miller's creative landscape and invites us to explore further the symbiotic relationship between Eastern philosophies and Western artistic expression.

The impact of modernism: breaking with traditional forms

The advent of modernism in literature marked a paradigm shift, challenging established conventions and redefining the boundaries of artistic expression. Basically, modernism sought to free itself from traditional forms and to innovate in terms of both content and style. This movement marked a break with the linear narratives and conventional structures that had dominated literature for centuries, placing the emphasis on introspection, fragmentation and experimentation. Writers abandoned chronological narrative in favour of non-linear narratives, fragmented plots and stream-of-consciousness techniques, inviting readers to engage with texts in non-traditional ways. In doing so, modernist writers sought to capture the complexities and ambiguities of human experience, reflecting the rapidly changing social, political and cultural landscapes of the early twentieth century. The modernist impulse extended beyond literature, permeating art, music and philosophy, fostering a holistic reimagining of creative expression. As a result, readers encountered works that defied their expectations, challenging them to confront uncertainty, abstraction and the absence of clear resolutions. The impact of modernism reverberated across all continents, influencing a wide range of writers who found inspiration in the movement's bold spirit of reinvention.

Literary kinship: James Joyce and symbolic subversion

In exploring Henry Miller's literary universe, it is essential to recognise the profound influence of James Joyce and his revolutionary approach to narrative structure and linguistic experimentation. The bond between Miller and Joyce goes beyond simple admiration; it is a shared commitment to questioning societal norms and unravelling the complexities of human consciousness.

James Joyce's magnum opus, 'Ulysses', is a testament to his unrivalled ability to deconstruct traditional forms of narrative and language. Using stream-of-consciousness, complex wordplay and radical narrative techniques, Joyce created a novel that defied conventional expectations and redefined the possibilities of literature. His work not only reflected the changing realities of an evolving world, it also served as an example of artistic rebellion against stagnation and complacency.

Miller's literary work bears the indelible stamp of Joyce's innovative spirit. In novels such as Tropic of Cancer and Tropic of Capricorn, Miller echoes Joyce's penchant for weaving multiple narrative threads and revelling in the chaotic symphony of everyday existence. Moreover, both writers share a penchant for symbolic subversion, using their prose not only as a means of storytelling, but also as a platform for dismantling established societal constructs and engaging in a relentless quest for truth.

Moreover, the thematic resonances between Joyce and Miller are unmistakable. Both authors grapple with the nuances of human experience, from the sordid underbelly of urban life to the transcendental potential of individual consciousness. Their works are labyrinths of meaning that invite readers to participate in a collective journey of intellectual discovery and self-revelation.

The kinship between James Joyce and Henry Miller goes beyond mere literary admiration and constitutes a symbiotic relationship characterised by parallel quests for artistic expression and existential understanding. As we delve deeper into Miller's work, we must continually acknowledge the profound impact of James Joyce on his literary development and the enduring legacy of their shared commitment to artistic innovation and symbolic subversion.

Artistic symbiosis: Picasso and changing realities

The partnership between literature and the visual arts has a deep history, with each influencing and reflecting the other to produce new ideas. In the same way that Tropic of Cancer challenged literary conventions, Picasso's revolutionary approach to art reshaped visual expression. The convergence of these two avant-garde giants unleashed an era of creative effervescence and intellectual cross-pollination, enriching both disciplines in unprecedented ways.

Pablo Picasso, one of the most influential artists of the twentieth century, shattered traditional artistic boundaries with his pioneering Cubist movement. By deconstructing and reshaping forms and perspectives, Picasso challenged viewers to confront perception itself, in the same way that Henry Miller's disruptive narrative style shattered literary conventions. The interplay between visual and literary innovation led to mutual enrichment, as both artists sought to capture the essence of human experience and consciousness.

In their respective fields, Miller and Picasso embarked on a quest to depict the many facets of reality. While Miller used conscious prose to reveal the inner world of his characters, Picasso fragmented and reassembled visual elements to offer a new perspective on the external environment. The dialogue between their works opened up a space for interpretation, inviting the public to question and explore the shifting boundaries between reality and abstraction, form and chaos.

Moreover, just as Miller's narratives often embraced themes of sexuality, desire and primal energy, Picasso's art boldly engaged with similar primal forces. His expressive use of colour, form and composition infuses his paintings with raw emotional power and energy, echoing the uninhibited spirit that characterises Miller's literary rebellion. This fusion of emotional fervour and intellectual vigour resulted in an aesthetic revolution that transcended categories and genres, leaving an indelible mark on the trajectory of modern art and literature.

Together, Miller and Picasso formed a symbiotic relationship that transcended the boundaries of different media, demonstrating the interconnectedness of artistic vision across diverse forms of expression. Their innovative approaches continue to reverberate in contemporary culture, inspiring future generations to question artistic norms, push the boundaries of perception and seek new dimensions of truth and understanding.

Psychoanalysis and creativity: Jungian archetypes in literature

When considering the complex relationship between psychoanalysis and creativity, it is impossible to ignore the profound influence of Jungian archetypes in literature. Carl Gustav Jung, the eminent Swiss psychiatrist, not only pioneered analytical psychology, but also exerted a lasting influence on the world of literature through his concept of archetypes. These primordial symbols and universal themes, rooted in the collective unconscious, have provided writers with a rich tapestry of motifs and stories.

Jung's theory of archetypes resonates deeply with the creative process, providing a framework for understanding the recurring patterns found in myths, fairy tales and literature across diverse cultures and eras. From the heroic journey of the 'hero' archetype to the transformative power of the 'magician', these archetypes offer a timeless reservoir of inspiration for writers seeking to imbue their work with depth and resonance.

Moreover, the exploration of Jungian archetypes reveals the interconnectedness of human experience, inviting readers to connect with characters and stories at a fundamental, often subconscious, level. By tapping into these archetypal motifs, writers can transcend the boundaries of personal narrative, touching on elemental truths that have universal resonance.

The integration of Jungian archetypes into literature not only enriches the narrative landscape, but also serves as a catalyst for individual and collective introspection. The characters who embody the archetypes become vessels that explore the human psyche, confront existential dilemmas and navigate the complexities of human existence. Whether it's the obscure depths of the 'Trickster' or the inherent wisdom of the 'Wise Old Man', these archetypes act as mirrors reflecting the countless facets of the human condition.

Moreover, the use of Jungian archetypes imbues literary works with layers of symbolism and allegory, transcending the immediate plot to convey deeper philosophical and psychological themes. By invoking archetypal imagery and motifs, authors engage in a subtle dialogue with the collective unconscious, inviting readers to embark on a profound journey of self-discovery and introspection.

Ultimately, the integration of Jungian archetypes into literature serves as a bridge between individual expression and collective understanding, bridging the gap between personal creativity and universal meaning. By tapping into these primitive symbols and innate themes, writers have an unparalleled opportunity to create narratives that resonate across cultural and temporal barriers, evoking a profound sense of recognition and enrichment in their audience.

Music as metaphor: jazz, freedom and formlessness

The influence of music on literature, and in particular the profound impact of jazz, is a subject well worth exploring. Just as jazz musicians improvise and mix different musical elements to create something new and dynamic, writers often draw parallels between the free nature of jazz and the literary expression of freedom and formlessness. Jazz, with its emphasis on improvisation and spontaneous creativity, serves as a metaphor for the unstructured, experimental approach adopted by many writers at the same time. The syncopated rhythms and dissonant chords of jazz find their equivalents in the unconventional narrative structures and discordant themes prevalent in avant-garde literature.

Moreover, the thematic links between jazz and literature are profound. Both art forms have been confronted with the expression of identity, societal constraints and the quest for individuality. The improvised nature of jazz reflects the way in which some writers have sought to break free from traditional literary conventions, engaging in linguistic innovation and adopting a stream-of-consciousness style akin to jazz improvisation. It is not uncommon for authors to use jazz as an intertextual reference, weaving its spirit into their narratives to capture the essence of personal and collective liberation.

Moreover, the concept of freedom inherent in jazz resonates with the thematic explorations found in literature. Writers have often turned to jazz to convey the complexities of human experience, reflecting the genre's ability to encapsulate raw emotions and existential aspirations. This parallel is evident in the way authors have used jazz motifs, integrating them into their prose to evoke a sense of fluidity and spontaneity, imbuing their work with the same sense of rhythm, syncopation and improvisation that defines the genre itself.

In addition, the thematic association between jazz and literature extends to the representation of urban life and the African-American experience. Jazz, particularly during the Harlem Renaissance, served as a vehicle for expressing the unique social realities and cultural expressions of black communities. Similarly, the literature of the period reflected these experiences, delving into the nuances of race, identity and the struggle for self-expression. The symbiotic relationship between jazz and literature thus becomes emblematic of a shared trajectory towards artistic emancipation and cultural redefinition.

Ultimately, the intertwining of jazz and literature affirms the indelible links between the art forms, illustrating how they have perpetually inspired and informed each other. As such, exploring this relationship provides a deeper understanding of the creative processes and thematic concerns that defined an era of artistic innovation and subversion.

Cinematic influences: visual narrative and temporal fluidity

The influence of film on literature is a subject of enduring fascination, as the intersection of visual narrative and temporal fluidity offers a rich tapestry to explore. When examining the impact of cinematic influences on literary works, the deep connection between the two art forms should not be underestimated. Cinematic storytelling, with its ability to convey a narrative through visual and aural means, has permeated the fabric of modern literature, infusing it with new techniques and perspectives. From the avant-garde experimentation of early filmmakers to the construction of an immersive world by contemporary authors, the parallels between the two mediums are undeniable. The power of the moving image to evoke emotion, stimulate the imagination and challenge conventional narratives is a force to be reckoned with.

While literature seeks to capture the essence of human experience, the influence of film provides a compelling framework for expressing the complexities of existence. Writers have found inspiration in the non-linear structures, manipulation of time and visual symbolism used in film. Just as montage has revolutionised the way stories are told on screen, it has also influenced the fragmentation and juxtaposition of narrative elements in literature. In addition, the concept of temporal fluidity, as exemplified in films that play with chronology and perception, has stimulated literary experimentation with non-linear timelines, parallel narratives and shifting perspectives. The symbiosis between literature and film extends beyond narrative techniques to encompass thematic explorations.

Cinematic motifs such as the hero's journey, the duality of identity and the subjective nature of reality have found an echo in literary landscapes, enriching the representation of human struggles and triumphs. In addition, the visual grammar of cinema, including framing, lighting and staging, encouraged authors to incorporate vivid images and sensory experiences into their prose, transcending the traditional boundaries of written language. It is in this dynamic interaction between literature and film that the boundaries of artistic expression become blurred, opening the way to a renaissance of creative possibilities. By delving into the influences of film on literature, we discover a dialogue between the two mediums that transcends mere adaptation or homage, forging a symbiotic relationship that reinvigorates the narrative traditions of both fields. The echoes of cinematic innovation resonate in the pages of modern literature, propelling stories to new heights of visual dynamism and temporal elasticity.

11

Literary Legacy
Impact and Influence on the Beat Generation

Tracing influences and impact

Henry Miller's literary career was deeply intertwined with the cultural landscape of the 1940s and 1950s, a period characterised by post-war disillusionment, social upheaval and shifting artistic paradigms. To understand Miller's legendary impact on the Beat Generation, it is imperative to delve into the influences that shaped his own writing. Exploring the literary environment of this period reveals a dynamic milieu brimming with experimentation and dissent. Influential figures such as T.S. Eliot, D.H. Lawrence and Walt Whitman left an indelible imprint on Miller's budding sensibility, infusing his work with a rawness and fervour that resonated with those disillusioned with societal norms.

Indeed, their radical approaches to form and content served as catalysts for Miller's departure from conventional narrative, heralding a new era of unbridled expression and introspection. In addition, existential philosophers such as Friedrich Nietzsche and Henri Bergson provided him with intellectual support, developing in him a profound sense of individualism and a rejection of dogmatic authority. This heterogeneous tapestry of influences converged in Miller's work, giving rise to a body of work that challenges dominant literary traditions and dogmas, provoking controversy and fascination in equal measure. In particular, Miller's adoption of a run-of-the-mill narrative and frank exploration of taboo subjects reflects the beat ethos, anticipating the counter-cultural revolution that would unfold over the following decades. By tracing these influences, it becomes clear that Miller's impact on the Beat Generation is not simply the product of chronological proximity; rather, it emanates from a shared spirit of defiance against institutionalised mediocrity and a yearning for existential authenticity. With this understanding of context, we are ready to embark on a nuanced exploration of Miller's enduring influence on the voices that emerged in the wake of his radical literary odyssey.

The literary environment of the 1940s and 1950s

The literary landscape of the 1940s and 1950s witnessed a seismic shift in artistic expression, particularly within American literature. This era marked the emergence of unconventional voices seeking to break free from the constraints of traditional narrative structures and societal norms. Writers were forced to explore new and uncharted territory, inspired by the revolutionary fervour of post-war disillusionment and social upheaval. In this context of effervescence and tumult, Henry Miller found himself in the vanguard of a literary revolution, challenging prevailing conventions with his frank and provocative prose. The cultural climate of the time favoured rebellion against established literary traditions. It was a period when writers sought to dismantle the boundaries of censorship and propriety, opting instead to defend raw authenticity and unfettered creativity.

The Beat Generation, in particular, emerged as a radical response to the perceived limitations of traditional literature. Driven by an ardent desire for individualistic expression, the writers of this generation embarked on a quest to unravel the complexities of human experience while exploring the uncharted territories of the human psyche. This era saw the flowering of experimental poetry, revealing memoirs and groundbreaking novels that shed light on the many facets of human existence. In this rapidly changing milieu, Miller's contributions testify to the power of unvarnished storytelling, challenging conventional literary norms and captivating audiences with his uncompromising approach.

The 1940s and 1950s thus provided fertile ground for the germination of literary movements that would irrevocably alter the course of American letters. It was a time when the written word transcended its usual boundaries, leading to an intellectual and creative renaissance that continues to reverberate in contemporary literature. Through their unwavering commitment to articulating pure truth and embracing the dynamism of language, writers of this era charted a new trajectory for artistic innovation, forever altering the tapestry of literary history.

Miller's radical departure from traditional prose

Henry Miller's literary impact goes far beyond his thematic content; his structural break with traditional prose forever altered the landscape of modern literature. By challenging the established conventions of his time, Miller challenged the limits of narrative and form, ushering in a new era of creativity and free expression. By embarking on this radical path, Miller paved the way for future generations of writers to free themselves from the constraints of traditional literary architecture, adopting a more authentic and experimental approach to storytelling. Miller's works, particularly 'Tropic of Cancer' and 'Tropic of Capricorn', introduced a stream-of-consciousness narrative style that moved away from linear chronology and coherence, favouring instead a raw, unfiltered description of human experience. This break with traditional prose reflects not only the chaotic and fragmented nature of existence, but also the inner turmoil and introspection prevalent in his time. Through this unconventional approach, Miller sought to capture the essence of life in its tumultuous and unrefined state, eliciting deep emotional responses from his readers.

The unabashed depiction of taboo subjects, explicit language and visceral imagery illustrates Miller's fearless rejection of societal norms, eliciting both scandal and acclaim. Moreover, by incorporating autobiographical elements into his fiction, Miller blurred the boundaries between fact and fiction, inviting readers to question the nature of truth and the limits of literary form itself. His radical break with traditional prose also lay in his refusal to adhere to conventional morality, celebrating the hedonistic and anarchic aspects of human existence. In doing so, he embraced the full spectrum of human experience, exposing the raw, primal instincts that lie dormant within us all. This departure had a lasting impact on the evolution of literature, inspiring subsequent generations of writers to embrace their authenticity and challenge literary conventions. Miller's avant-garde approach has left an indelible mark on the literary world, continuing to influence and inspire writers who seek to challenge and redefine the boundaries of artistic expression.

Symbolism and themes addressed by Beat Generation writers

The Beat Generation, often described as a literary movement centred on counter-culture ideals, embraced a myriad of symbols and deep-seated themes that resonated with a wide audience. Beat Generation writers sought to challenge societal norms and traditional values, advocating personal freedom and self-expression. Themes of rebellion against conformity, spiritual exploration and the quest for individual authenticity are at the heart of their works. These profound themes served as powerful vehicles for conveying the philosophies and ideologies of the beats, captivating readers and inspiring future generations.

Symbolism abounded in their literature, with motifs such as the open road, jazz music, drug use and Eastern spirituality all embodying the search for liberation and truth. Kerouac's concept of 'spontaneous prose' and Ginsberg's confessional poetry became emblematic of the movement's rejection of formal structure and embrace of raw, unfiltered human experience. The beat generation's exploration of sexuality, addiction and existential angst challenged the dominant moral norms of the time and laid the foundations for frank and uninhibited artistic expression. This intrepid approach had a lasting impact on literature and popular culture, as evidenced by the works of subsequent generations of writers who continued to draw on the legacy of the 'beats'. The enduring influence of these themes and symbols on contemporary art, music and thought testifies to the depth and relevance of the Beat Generation's contributions to the cultural landscape.

In the field of literary history, Henry Miller's influence on the iconic figures of the Beat Generation - Jack Kerouac, Allen Ginsberg and William S. Burroughs - is profound and multifaceted. These luminaries, who went on to shape a counter-cultural movement that would influence generations to come, were deeply influenced by Miller's unabashed approach to writing about the human experience. The raw, unrestrained nature of Miller's prose served as a model for their own exploration of unconventional themes and unfiltered personal expression. Kerouac, often regarded as the pioneer of the spontaneous prose style, found inspiration in Miller's fearless disregard for literary convention. This influence is evident in Kerouac's seminal works,

The challenge to morality and conventional society

Henry Miller's literary works, notably 'Tropic of Cancer' and 'Tropic of Capricorn', are characterised by an unflinching confrontation with societal norms and conventional morality. In these groundbreaking novels, Miller fearlessly tackles taboo subjects such as sexuality, existential angst and the alienation of the individual in modern society. In doing so, he not only challenged prevailing moral codes, but also exposed the injustices and hypocrisies inherent in societal structures.

Miller's exploration of sexual liberation and eroticism was revolutionary for its time, representing a direct affront to Puritan values and the restrictive censorship that prevailed in literature. Her outspoken depiction of human sexuality and desire sparked fervent debate about artistic freedom and the limits of acceptable expression. Rather than conforming to societal expectations, Miller fearlessly depicts the raw, unfiltered reality of human experience, inviting readers to confront the complexities of desire and intimacy without reservation.

Moreover, Miller's critique extended beyond the realm of personal relationships, encompassing a broader dissection of societal constructs. He laid bare the disparity between the idealised façade of civilisation and the stark and often disheartening realities of existence. With vivid, uncompromising prose, he showed the underbelly of urban life, where characters grapple with disillusionment, poverty and alienation. His characters were not mere archetypes, but representatives of the disenfranchised and the disenchanted - a bold portrayal that both resonated with and unsettled readers.

Moreover, Miller's challenge to conventional morality extended to a poignant indictment of materialism, consumerism and the dehumanising effects of modernity. His critique of societal values spilled over into the Beats, inspiring a countercultural movement that sought to reject conformity and embrace authenticity. The subversive nature of Miller's writing prompted readers to question the status quo, triggering a cultural awakening that permeated literature, art and social discourse for generations to come.

In essence, Miller's work is an enduring testament to the invincible spirit of individualism and the relentless pursuit of truth in the face of moral and societal constraints. His fearless art continues to inspire and provoke, compelling readers to re-examine their beliefs, confront their inhibitions and contemplate the transformative power of unbridled expression.

Criticism and censorship: parallels in reception

Critics and censorship have played a key role in the reception and legacy of Henry Miller's work, drawing fascinating parallels with the experiences of Beat Generation writers. The controversial nature of Miller's prose provoked strong reactions from literary critics and authorities, who often deemed his writings obscene and unfit for public consumption, leading to censorship attempts and legal battles. Similarly, Beat writers, including Jack Kerouac, Allen Ginsberg and William S. Burroughs, faced similar challenges because of their unconventional and unabashedly crude narratives, which challenged societal norms and values.

Miller's pioneering use of explicit language and depictions of sexuality clashed with prevailing moral standards, sparking passionate debates about artistic freedom and the limits of literature. His novels, notably Tropic of Cancer and Tropic of Capricorn, were fiercely opposed, resulting in bans and confiscations in several countries. The Beats met with similar resistance, as their bold exploration of counter-cultural themes and open discussion of taboo subjects provoked widespread controversy and condemnation.

The convergence of critical scorn and censorship intensified the mystique surrounding the works of Miller and the Beat writers, propelling them to the forefront of rebellious literary movements. Their defiance of societal conventions and refusal to adhere to mainstream expectations cemented their reputations as provocative figures who challenged the status quo, exposing the hypocrisies of a censored society.

Moreover, the controversial reception of Miller and the Beats provoked impassioned defences from defenders of free speech and artistic expression, sparking fervent dialogues about the role of literature in reflecting and critiquing human experience. The legal battles that followed provided a battleground for fundamental questions about the right of authors to convey the truth as they see it, unhindered by external judgements and interference.

Ultimately, the enduring influence of Miller and the writers of the Beat Generation underlines the ability of art to transcend stifling constraints and assert itself in the face of attempts to stifle its dissemination. Their unwavering commitment to authenticity and unbridled expression continues to resonate with contemporary audiences, reaffirming the power of literature to subvert, challenge and inspire, despite the obstacles placed in its path.

Philosophical principles shared with the Beats

The philosophical underpinnings of Henry Miller's works resonate deeply with the ideals embraced by the Beat Generation. Both Miller and the Beats rejected societal norms and traditional values, seeking to redefine existence on their own terms. At the heart of their shared philosophy was a rejection of materialism and consumerism, in favour of a more authentic and experimental approach to life. This disdain for the superficial and commercial is reflected in Miller's writings and echoed in the works of Beat icons such as Jack Kerouac, Allen Ginsberg and William S. Burroughs. Their collective yearning for spiritual fulfilment and transcendence is evident in Miller's existential explorations. The Beats' emphasis on personal freedom and unfettered expression reflects Miller's fervent belief in the liberation of the individual from societal constraints.

Both Miller and the Beats portrayed a visceral and unfiltered perspective on life, rejecting conventional morality and embracing the rawness of human experience. In addition, the Eastern philosophical influences apparent in Miller's work, notably his fascination with Zen Buddhism, resonated within the Beat community. This convergence of Eastern thought with rebellious, counter-cultural attitudes gave rise to a shared ethos that transcended geographical and generational boundaries. Moreover, Miller's relentless quest for authenticity and truth, exemplified by his honest and uncompromising portrayal of human desires and shortcomings, resonated with the Beats' rejection of the hypocrisy and artificiality of mainstream society. Finally, both Miller and the Beats demonstrated a remarkable rejection of literary convention, opting for a spontaneous prose and unbridled narrative style that reflected the stream-of-consciousness writing prevalent in Beat literature. As a result, Miller's impact on the Beat Generation goes beyond mere thematic similarities; it permeates their fundamental approach to life, art and self-expression.

The legacy in contemporary literature and culture

Henry Miller's impact on contemporary literature and culture is profound and extends far beyond his own generation. As the Beat Generation evolved into the countercultural movements of the 1960s and the literary waves that followed, the impact of Miller's uninhibited prose and radical worldview continued to be felt. His unreserved embrace of taboo subjects and unfiltered exploration of the human experience have left an indelible mark on the landscape of modern literature.

One of the key elements of Miller's legacy is his challenge to the status quo. By fearlessly tackling themes such as sexuality, spirituality and societal norms, Miller inspired future generations of writers to push boundaries and challenge convention. The raw authenticity of his work and his refusal to censor his thoughts or experiences have had a lasting impact on contemporary literary expression, allowing writers to delve into the depths of the human psyche and confront uncomfortable truths with honesty and vulnerability.

Miller's influence extends beyond the realm of literature. His relentless critique of consumerist culture and rejection of materialism resonated with the countercultural movements of the 1960s and 1970s, influencing the emerging ethos of anti-establishment thought and activism. Artists, musicians and thinkers drawn to the spirit of rebellion found inspiration in Miller's fervent rejection of societal norms and embraced his call for a more authentic and liberated existence.

In contemporary literature, Miller's legacy can be seen in the works of authors who continue to challenge traditional narrative structures and societal mores. Writers who explore the complexities of human desire, personal freedom and the search for meaning are indebted to Miller's bold experiments with form and content. His willingness to confront the darker aspects of human nature and the contradictions inherent in the human condition has provided fertile ground for contemporary writers who seek to capture the complexities of existence with unwavering honesty.

Miller's influence is also evident in the fluidity of genres and the dissolution of artistic boundaries in modern literature. His rejection of rigid categorisations and his fearless blending of autobiographical elements and fictional narratives have encouraged contemporary writers to break free from traditional constraints and explore the intersection of reality and imagination. As a result, Miller's impact on contemporary literature extends beyond mere stylistic emulation to a fundamental reimagining of the possibilities inherent in narrative and self-expression.

The enduring relevance of Henry Miller's literary work and the resonance of his ideas in contemporary culture underscore the depth of his legacy. His unwavering commitment to truth-telling and his unshakeable belief in the transformative power of art continue to inspire and provoke writers and readers alike, ensuring that his influence will endure for generations to come.

Conclusion: Lasting imprints on a generation

Henry Miller's literary legacy extends far beyond his immediate influence on the Beat Generation, leaving indelible marks on subsequent generations of writers, thinkers and cultural icons. His raw, candid writing style, which challenged societal norms and conventional morality, ushered in a new era of literary expression. By fearlessly plunging into the depths of human experience and embracing the chaos of existence, Miller unleashed a literary revolution that transcended geographical and cultural boundaries.

Miller's impact on the Beat Generation was profound, inspiring a group of visionary writers such as Jack Kerouac, Allen Ginsberg and William S. Burroughs. Miller's radical departure from established literary norms, combined with his unbridled exploration of themes such as sexuality, spirituality and rebellion against authority, became emblematic of the Beat ethos. Miller's influence permeated their work, instilling a sense of liberation and rejection of societal constraints.

Moreover, Miller's philosophical principles, rooted in existentialism and a fervent celebration of individual freedom, resonated deeply with the fundamental principles espoused by the Beats. His writings served as both catalyst and manifesto for a generation seeking to break free from the shackles of conformity and embrace a life of unfettered authenticity. This philosophical synchronicity between Miller and the Beat writers laid the foundations for a cultural movement that would shape subsequent countercultural movements and ideologies.

The enduring relevance of Miller's work to contemporary literature and culture underlines the timeless nature of his ideas. His unflinching portrayal of the human condition, with its struggles, triumphs and complexities, continues to resonate with readers from diverse cultural backgrounds. From his evocative prose to his impassioned treatises on the art of living, Miller's artistic prowess is a testament to literature's enduring power to provoke, challenge and inspire.

As we navigate the complexities of the modern age, Miller's legacy remains a touchstone for those who seek to interrogate the truths of existence and confront the many facets of human experience. His ability to confront taboos, defy convention and celebrate the inherent beauty of life remains a beacon for those who dare to push the boundaries of artistic expression and engage in introspective contemplation.

In conclusion, Henry Miller's impact on the Beat Generation goes far beyond a mere literary influence. He shaped the very essence of a cultural and philosophical movement that continues to reverberate in the collective consciousness of contemporary society. His unwavering commitment to authenticity, his intrepid exploration of the human psyche and his unwavering dedication to the proliferation of artistic freedom are enduring testaments to the transformative power of literature.

12

Letters and Essays

Insight into the Human Condition

Miller's art of letter writing

The art of letter writing occupies a prominent place in Henry Miller's literary work, serving as a channel for introspective exploration and frank expression. Miller's approach to correspondence transcends mere communication; it becomes a complex tapestry of thoughts, emotions and revelations. Each missive reflects a deliberate composition, imbued with the raw essence of his experiences, impressions and philosophical reflections. Miller's letters, characterised by unabashed honesty and fervent introspection, invite readers into the inner sanctum of his conscience, forging an intimate bond between author and recipient. This epistolary art illustrates Miller's commitment to capturing the pulsating rhythms of life through the written word, elevating the act of correspondence to an art form that reflects the tumultuous pace of existence.

In the context of Miller's work, his letters are not relegated to mere personal exchanges; rather, they serve as autonomous literary works, embodying profound reflections on the human condition and the interconnectedness of creative endeavour. The visceral, unmediated nature of Miller's epistolary style radiates an unparalleled authenticity that reverberates through the annals of time. As a keen observer of human experience, Miller uses his epistolary art to navigate the complexities of existence, creating an enduring testament to the resilience of the human spirit and the kaleidoscopic nature of emotion. By highlighting his personal triumphs and struggles, Miller enriches the legacy of the epistolary tradition, breathing new life into a timeless mode of expression. In this way, the exploration of Miller's epistolary art reveals a symbiotic relationship between the reflexive nature of epistolary writing and the evolution of literary prowess, immersing readers in a world where the boundaries between personal revelations and universal truths dissolve, leaving behind a palpable essence that resonates with resounding depth.

The role of letters in creative writing

In the field of creative writing, letters have a profound significance as instruments for crossing the boundaries between thought and expression. Henry Miller's masterful use of letters as a form of literary craft is emblematic of his ability to harness the power of intimate communication to evoke emotion, provoke thought and inspire storytelling. The epistolary form, with its inherent sense of immediacy and authenticity, allows Miller to shed pretense and delve into the raw essence of human experience. By employing this mode of communication, he creates an intimate dialogue with his readers, drawing them into the deepest workings of his mind and soul.
This direct, unfiltered approach lays bare the complexities of his inner world, fostering a deep connection between author and audience. In this way, Miller transcends simple narrative and achieves a profound exploration of the human condition. The letters become vessels through which

the subtleties of human emotion, the turbulence of personal relationships and the wider societal context are conveyed with unparalleled sincerity and depth. They provide an unvarnished means of expressing joy, sadness, love and despair - universal themes that resonate across time and cultural divides. In addition, the epistolary form allows Miller to experiment with narrative structure, blurring the boundaries between fiction and reality. Through the interplay of letters and literary imagination, he creates a rich tapestry of interconnected experiences that blurs the boundaries of traditional narrative, inviting readers to embark on a journey that is both deeply personal and universally relevant. As such, letters not only convey the subjective truths of individual lives, but also open windows onto the wider canvas of human experience. In the hands of an artist such as Miller, letters transcend their utilitarian purpose and become powerful tools of introspection, revelation and transcendence. By revealing the emotional, intellectual and philosophical landscapes of his correspondence, Miller elevates the epistolary form to an art form that captures the nuances and complexities of the human psyche. By skilfully manipulating language, imagery and sentiment, Miller imbues each letter with a profound literary resonance, transforming them into contemplative mirrors that reflect the many facets of the human soul.

Themes of solitude and companionship

Henry Miller's exploration of the human condition deepens the themes of solitude and companionship. In his letters and essays, he vividly portrays the dichotomy between the individual's desire for solitude and the fundamental need for meaningful human relationships. Through introspective prose and poignant reflections, Miller captures the essence of the human experience in solitude and companionship.

For Miller, solitude is not just a physical state, but a profound existential condition. In his correspondence and essays, he addresses the loneliness that permeates the human soul. He stresses the importance of solitude as a catalyst for introspection, creative contemplation and spiritual awakening. Miller's image of solitude transcends mere isolation, describing it as an essential space for the individual to confront his or her deepest thoughts, fears and desires. Through his writings, he elucidates the transformative power of solitude, emphasising its role in self-discovery and personal fulfilment.

Conversely, Miller is also interested in the complex dynamics of companionship and the search for meaningful human connections. He eloquently describes the yearning for true companionship and emotional intimacy in a world of superficial interactions. Through his essays, he examines the many forms of companionship, from platonic friendships to romantic relationships, and paints an intimate portrait of the human yearning for authentic connection. Miller's insightful commentary on companionship reveals the inherent vulnerabilities and profound joys that flow from human relationships, highlighting the universal quest for mutual understanding and emotional resonance.

Moreover, Miller's exploration of loneliness and companionship is interwoven with a keen observation of societal norms and cultural constructs. His astute analysis explores the impact of societal expectations on individual experiences of loneliness and companionship, highlighting the complexities of human interaction within the wider context of social and cultural frameworks. Through thought-provoking narratives and insightful perspectives, Miller invites readers to discern the complex interplay between personal autonomy, societal pressures and the search for authentic connection.

In essence, Miller's depiction of solitude and companionship resonates with profound relevance, offering illuminating insights into the human desire for introspection, connection and belonging. His evocative portrait is a timeless testament to the eternal quest for meaning and fulfilment in human relationships.

Social commentary through essays

In his compelling essays, Henry Miller paints a vivid and unflinchingly honest portrait of the social landscape. Through his keen observations and introspective reflections, Miller tackles a myriad of social issues, encouraging readers to engage in critical reflection on the human condition. His penetrating commentary navigates the complexities of human interaction, societal norms and the struggle for authenticity in an increasingly mechanised world.

A recurring theme in Miller's essays is the exploration of the dissonance between individual aspirations and societal expectations. He explores the tension between conformity and rebellion, prompting contemplation of the nature of human agency and the pursuit of personal freedom in the midst of prevailing cultural constraints. Moreover, Miller fearlessly examines the hypocrisies and injustices embedded in societal structures, prompting readers to re-evaluate the role they play in perpetuating or challenging these systems.

Miller also uses the power of her lyrical voice to weave poignant narratives that serve as a critique of societal disparities and inequalities. Her essays reveal the harsh realities faced by marginalised communities and individuals, giving voice to those who are silenced and forgotten. Through rich and evocative prose, Miller forces readers to confront uncomfortable truths and empathise with the struggles of others, sparking a collective empathy that transcends geographical and cultural boundaries. His searing denunciations of social and economic hierarchies are calls for justice and solidarity.

Miller also uses his essays as a platform to explore the complex tapestry of human relationships and the impact of societal constructs on interpersonal dynamics. Through astute characterisation and insightful analysis, he reveals the complex interplay of love, power and desire within the social framework. His writings challenge conventional notions of romance, friendship and family ties, illuminating the nuanced complexities that underlie these relational aspects. Miller's essays thus provoke a thought-provoking discourse on the complexities of human connection and the transformative power of authentic emotional engagement.

Ultimately, Miller's essays demonstrate his unwavering commitment to seeking the truth about human experience. Through his incisive social commentary, he encourages readers to critically examine the state of the world and their place in it, urging them to introspect and advocate for positive change. By seamlessly blending literary prowess and socio-cultural knowledge, Miller's essays remain timeless articulations of the human condition.

The lyrical voice: poetic prose

Henry Miller's literary work is imbued with a lyrical voice that transcends traditional prose and delves deeply into the realm of poetic expression. His unique style, characterised by raw honesty and unbridled sensuality, evokes an emotional resonance that lingers in the hearts and minds of readers. With his mastery of language and imagery, Miller brings to life a world brimming with vitality, where the mundane becomes extraordinary and the profane is transformed into the sacred.

Miller's exploration of the human experience is a marriage of poetic sensibility and profound philosophical vision. His prose dances and sways like a melody, weaving together the rhythms of everyday life and the complexities of existence. With his vivid descriptions and evocative language, Miller invites us to see the world through a different lens - one that celebrates the beauty of imperfection and revels in the chaos of human emotion.

What sets Miller's poetic prose apart is that it fearlessly embraces the taboo and the unconventional. He fearlessly plunges into the depths of human desire, exposing the raw, unfiltered essence of our most primal instincts. In doing so, he challenges societal norms and the boundaries of traditional morality, inviting readers to question the concepts that define our understanding of love, passion and identity.

Moreover, Miller's poetic prose goes beyond mere personal expression; it serves as a vehicle for introspection and self-discovery. Through his contemplative musings and introspective narrative, he encourages readers to embark on their own journey of exploration, to delve into the recesses of their consciousness and confront the fundamental questions that define the human condition.

In essence, Miller's lyrical voice embodies a universal yearning for connection and understanding. It evokes the inherent yearning for authenticity and true human connection, transcending temporal and cultural boundaries. Through her poetic prose, Miller invites us to embrace the full spectrum of human experience - agony and ecstasy, darkness and light - and to find meaning and beauty in the complex tapestry of life.

Reflections on society and culture

In 'Reflections on Society and Culture', Henry Miller delves into the complex web of human interactions, societal structures and cultural nuances that shape the world around us. With a keen sense of observation and an unyielding commitment to frank expression, Miller sifts through the paradigms and conventions that govern human behaviour and relationships. Through his introspective lens, he uncovers layers of complexity in social dynamics, illuminating the multifaceted nature of community, identity and belonging. Miller's exploration of societal and cultural phenomena transcends mere observation; it embodies a profound contemplation of the human experience in all its richness and contradictions.

At the heart of Miller's reflections is a profound curiosity about the subtleties of human society. He skilfully dissects the different facets of social life, from the great tapestries of urban civilisation to the intimate subtleties of interpersonal relationships. Mixing personal anecdotes, historical references and philosophical reflections, Miller constructs a captivating narrative that invites readers to reconsider their own place in the social fabric. Moreover, his astute analyses challenge prevailing notions of conformity and tradition, encouraging individuals to chart their own course within the collective consciousness.

Miller also navigates the complex terrain of cultural expression and influence with remarkable insight. He celebrates the diversity of artistic expression in different societies, recognising the profound imprint that cultural heritage leaves on the human psyche. By examining the resonance of literature and art and probing the undercurrents of societal norms, Miller develops a thought-provoking discourse that encourages readers to re-evaluate their perceptions of cultural authenticity and innovation.

Throughout 'Reflections on Society and Culture', readers are invited to confront the tensions and harmonies inherent in the human condition. Miller's treatment of these themes is characterised by a rare combination of intellectual rigour and poignant sensitivity, offering a nuanced description of the interaction between the individual and the collective. Ultimately, this chapter is an invitation to embrace the complexities of human society and culture, inspiring a deeper understanding of the intricate tapestry that binds humanity together.

Philosophical reflections: The essential questions of life

Against the tumultuous backdrop of the twentieth century, Miller tackled timeless questions that have plagued humanity for centuries. He confronted the enigma of existence, the nature of reality and the purpose of human endeavour with a keen and unyielding intelligence. Miller embarked on a fervent quest to unravel the complexities of human consciousness, sincerely questioning the meaning of life and the underlying structure of the universe. Through introspective prose and incisive observations, he has plumbed the depths of the human condition, uncovering profound insights and highlighting the interconnectedness of all living things. His reflections go beyond mere contemplation; they serve as a catalyst for readers to confront their own existential questions and embark on a journey of self-discovery and enlightenment. By philosophising about the fundamental complexities of human existence, Miller invites readers to reflect on the ephemeral nature of time, the enigma of mortality and the perpetual quest for meaning.

With eloquent articulation that is both passionate and insightful, Miller navigates the labyrinthine corridors of metaphysical inquiry, forcing readers to confront their own beliefs, preconceptions and convictions about the world and their place in it. By exploring the essential questions of life, Miller invites us to contemplate the unchanging truths and enduring mysteries that transcend individual experience, providing an opportunity for deep introspection and intellectual discourse. As we accompany Miller on this cerebral odyssey, we are challenged to confront our inherent prejudices, reassess our perspectives and contemplate the universal implications of our own existence. By delving into the realms of philosophy, Miller elevates discourse beyond the mundane and taps into the collective consciousness of humanity, igniting a passionate flame of contemplative dialogue and existential introspection.

The influence of correspondence on narrative style

Henry Miller's literary work bears witness to the transformative power of personal correspondence in shaping his distinctive narrative style. The profound impact of letters exchanged with friends, mentors and contemporaries reverberates throughout his works, infusing them with a raw authenticity and unfiltered intimacy that transcends conventional narrative. By adopting the epistolary form, Miller offered his readers an unvarnished glimpse into his psyche, infusing his prose with a sense of urgency and immediacy. His correspondence became a source of creative inspiration, catalysing the development of an idiosyncratic narrative canvas that defied traditional literary conventions. The exchange of letters not only served as a crucible for the fermentation of ideas and themes, but also engendered a profound symbiosis between her personal life and her artistic expression. This convergence gave Miller's stories a deeply humanistic and palpable quality, eschewing artifice in favour of a visceral and emotional engagement with human experience. Drawing on the cadence of epistolary conversation, Miller imbues his stories with an uninhibited spontaneity, skilfully blending lucid introspection with fervent emotional outpourings. The tenor of the communication in his correspondence carries over into his stories, fostering an immersive, confessional narrative atmosphere that resonates with readers on a deeply personal level. As Miller danced across the boundaries of literary form, the epistolary undercurrents imbued his prose with an aura of candid revelation, allowing readers to partake in the reveries, passions and undisguised tribulations of a writer navigating the twists and turns of life and art. Moreover, the reciprocity inherent in epistolary exchange has influenced Miller's narrative rhythm, giving rise to an organic ebb and flow that reflects the dynamics of human interaction. This inherent dialogic quality has breathed vitality into his narratives, endowing them with an evocative dynamism that captures the ethos of interpersonal relationships. In this way, the letters indelibly etched into Miller's creative ethos have metamorphosed into the indispensable linchpin of his narrative alchemy, transforming his prose into an enduring testament to the existential contours of the human condition.

Introspection and the writer's journey

By immersing ourselves in the profound introspection of Henry Miller's letters and essays, we find ourselves on a transformative journey alongside the writer himself. In these introspective texts, Miller invites readers to explore the inner workings of his mind, offering a raw, unfiltered portrait of his personal experiences and philosophical reflections. The writer's journey mingles with the reader's quest for understanding and meaning, creating a symbiotic relationship that transcends the written word. Through introspection, Miller delves into the complexities of human existence, tackling universal themes of love, desire, alienation and the eternal quest for purpose. His candid exploration of the self is a poignant reminder of the inherent struggles and triumphs that define our common human condition. Moreover, the writer's journey goes beyond mere personal reflection; it becomes a vehicle for broader social and cultural critique. Miller's introspective narratives examine the intricate tapestry of societal norms, challenge convention and illuminate the often overlooked aspects of the human experience.

Through her introspective writing, Miller encourages readers to embark on their own journey of self-discovery and contemplation, provoking reflection and encouraging introspection. The transformative power of introspection is reflected in the evolution of Miller's literary style and themes. From the earliest letters to the latest reflective essays, we witness a shift in perspective and a deepening of insight as the writer grapples with the complexities of life. This evolving introspection not only enriches the narrative tapestry of Miller's works, but also leaves an indelible mark on the reader, igniting a spark of introspective contemplation that resonates long after the last page has been turned. In essence, the writer's journey through introspection serves as a testament to the enduring power of self-examination and exploration of the human psyche. As we traverse the landscapes of Miller's introspective narratives, we are reminded of our common humanity and the timeless quest for self-understanding. Through the writer's journey, we are invited to take part in a collective introspective odyssey, which offers solace, enlightenment and the timeless appeal of self-discovery.

The lasting impact of Miller's letters and essays

Henry Miller's letters and essays are timeless records of the human experience, offering a profound insight into the complexities of existence. Through his epistolary and essayistic art, Miller delved into the recesses of his own consciousness, embarking on a relentless exploration of himself and the world around him. As we journey through the landscapes of Miller's letters and essays, we are confronted with an irresistible mix of raw introspection and incisive commentary on the human condition. This lasting impact stems from Miller's unabashed authenticity and his unyielding commitment to depicting life in all its unvarnished reality.

In his letters, Miller invites readers into the sanctuary of his thoughts, baring his soul with an unwavering candour that resonates across time and space. Her correspondences are imbued with an emotional intensity that captures the essence of the human spirit, transcending the boundaries of time to forge bonds that transcend generations. The letters are windows into the tumultuous landscape of Miller's mind, chronicling his personal triumphs and tribulations, his loves and losses, and his relentless quest for artistic truth. Each missive is imbued with an indomitable vitality, breathing life into the pages and revealing enigmatic layers of Miller's psyche.

Moreover, Miller's essays illustrate his prowess as a keen observer of society and culture, using the written word as a powerful tool for social critique and introspective exploration. His essays take the reader into a world of contemplation and examination, where every line is a reservoir of intellectual stimulation and philosophical inquiry. Delving into the fundamentals of existence, Miller probes the very fabric of human nature, offering incisive reflections that resonate poignantly and universally. By combining intellectual acuity with visceral emotion, Miller's essays create a space for provocative discourse that remains as relevant today as it was when they were written.

The lasting impact of Miller's letters and essays reverberates through the corridors of literary history, leaving an indelible imprint on the collective consciousness of humanity. Their enduring relevance lies in their ability to encapsulate the essential truths of the human condition, truths that transcend ephemeral times and resonate with the perpetual quest for meaning and understanding. As we take leave of this exploration of Miller's epistolary and essayistic legacy, we do so with a new appreciation of the enriching depth they offer, reminding us that in the intimate contours of personal correspondence and the transformative power of the written word, we discover timeless treasures that illuminate the human experience.

13

Friends and Foes

Anaïs Nin and Literary Circles

Introduction to literary circles

Literary circles have long been recognised as crucibles for enriching discourse, nurturing talent and producing groundbreaking literary works. Budding writers often find solace, inspiration and camaraderie there, cultivating lifelong friendships and formidable creative partnerships. Indeed, the bohemian enclaves of Paris, New York and other artistic hotspots of the early twentieth century were hives of intellectual effervescence, where like-minded individuals gathered to discuss, debate and collaborate on the advancement of literary works.

The formation of these literary circles was not simply fortuitous but rather deliberate, often emerging from shared philosophical perspectives, aesthetic sensibilities or societal disillusionment. These associations transcended mere social groups, becoming incubators of radical ideas and avant-garde experimentation. Their impact has reverberated over the years, fundamentally shaping the course of literature and heralding new movements.

Within these circles, complex and often unconventional relationships have developed, giving rise to enduring creative partnerships that have redefined the landscape of modern literature. These relationships were characterised by mutual respect, intense intellectual engagement and a collective passion for artistic expression. The spirit of collaboration that reigned within these circles produced an abundance of innovative works that continue to inspire and provoke contemporary readers and writers.

Moreover, the influence of the literary circles extended beyond the realm of creative endeavour, manifesting itself in wider cultural, political and philosophical discourses. These intimate encounters allowed for the confluence of diverse ideologies, resulting in fervent discussion and mutual learning. Participation in these dynamic environments fuelled the intellectual and creative evolution of their participants, contributing to the emergence of literary titans and landmark works that remain timeless classics.

Exploring the multifaceted dynamics of literary circles invites us to delve into the intersection of individual genius and collaboration. It encourages us to contemplate the intricate tapestry of interpersonal connections that underlie the creation of literary masterpieces. By unravelling the essence of these circles, we gain invaluable insights into the interplay of creativity, camaraderie and catalytic influences that have forever altered the landscape of literature.

The seductive partnership : Henry and Anaïs

Henry Miller and Anaïs Nin shared a deep literary and personal connection that transcended conventional boundaries. Their partnership, characterised by intense intimacy and intellectual exchange, was a source of creative inspiration and emotional support for both writers. From the outset of their relationship, they recognised the potential for collaboration and mutual growth, paving the way for a transformative alliance in the field of literature. Their unconventional bond was fuelled by a deep understanding of each other's creative processes and a shared dedication to artistic expression. Despite the complexities and occasional turmoil that marked their intertwined lives, Miller and Nin forged an enduring partnership that has left an indelible mark on the landscape of modern literature. The dynamic interplay between their respective literary visions gave them the freedom to explore new avenues of thought and to break free from the constraints of societal norms. Their correspondence, filled with raw emotion and unfiltered revelations, testifies to the unparalleled depth of their bond, which goes beyond mere platonic or professional affiliations. Founded on a shared commitment to authenticity and uninhibited self-expression, their partnership has transcended the boundaries of traditional relationships, sparking a renaissance in their individual creative endeavours. Through the lens of their complex bond, Miller and Nin's intertwined narratives draw readers into a world where truth and art intersect with breathtaking candour. This chapter explores the nuances of their partnership, revealing the layers of influence and reciprocity that defined their extraordinary alliance.

By exploring their letters, diaries and joint works, we witness the fusion of two distinct voices that merge into a harmonious symphony of literary innovation. The appeal of their partnership lies not only in its impact on their personal lives, but also in the wider context of their contributions to the evolution of literature, testifying to the transformative power of genuine connection and creative symbiosis.

Facing adversity: friend or foe?

In the tumultuous landscape of literary history, some relationships have captured the imagination with their intensity and complexity. The dynamic bond between Henry Miller and Anaïs Nin is one of those exciting sagas that span the realms of camaraderie, collaboration and conflict. Their intertwined lives are marked by a current of emotional turbulence accompanied by artistic resonance. Amidst the lure of creativity, the question arises as to the true nature of their relationship: were they steadfast allies or belligerent adversaries?

On the surface, it's a bond forged in the crucible of shared literary ambitions and a deep mutual admiration for each other's work. Their interconnected stories paint a picture of unyielding devotion, but beneath this veneer of solidarity lie cracks created by personal differences and conflicting aspirations. Beneath the facade of friendly collaboration, Miller and Nin have both faced individual challenges and aspirations that have sometimes pitted them against each other. Their tumultuous love affair has infused their professional association with a volatile energy, oscillating between moments of creative synergy and discordant dissonance.

The complex web of their intertwined lives reveals a panorama riddled with moments of friction and conflict. Clashes of ego, power struggles and the relentless pursuit of artistic autonomy have all contributed to the tumultuous nature of their partnership. As they embarked on a journey marked by creative exchange and intellectual dialogue, the transformative power of their connection shaped the contours of their respective literary legacies. Themes of trust and betrayal resonate throughout the chapters of their shared narrative, inviting readers to ponder the enigmatic duality of their bond.

Nevertheless, amidst the stormy landscapes of their relationship, glimpses of deep understanding and unwavering support have emerged. Their interactions served as a crucible for spiritual and artistic development, fostering an environment where vulnerabilities could be exposed and points of view exchanged. Their shared experiences created a convoluted tapestry of emotions, blurring the boundaries between friendship and antagonism, collaboration and competition. It is in these murky depths that the essence of their connection, both tender and conflicted, finds its elusive resonance, perpetuating an enduring mystique that continues to fascinate and bewitch.

Unconventional stories: collaboration with Nin

The collaboration between Henry Miller and Anaïs Nin marked a milestone in the field of unconventional storytelling. Both renowned for their distinct literary voices, the convergence of their creative energies gave birth to a body of work that challenged the traditional norms of storytelling. Their partnership transcended conventional author-publisher relationships, evolving into a deep and complex artistic alliance shaped by mutual respect and admiration. Through this collaboration, Miller and Nin inaugurated an innovative narrative style that blurs the boundaries between fiction and reality, inviting readers to plunge into the raw, unfiltered depths of human experience. Embracing the complexities of love, desire and existential angst, their combined works challenge society's taboos and explore the intricate nuances of human relationships. This union of literary minds has introduced a new dimension to storytelling, weaving intimate revelations and provocative introspection into the fabric of their narratives. The unconventional nature of their collaboration has continued to inspire and intrigue literary scholars, offering profound insights into the transformative power of art and its ability to reflect the human condition. In this way, the legacy of their collaboration testifies to the lasting impact of bold and unorthodox storytelling in the annals of literary history.

The bohemian bond between Anaïs Nin and Henry Miller transcended conventional norms, hinging on a shared commitment to artistic freedom, emotional authenticity and unabashed self-expression. Their bond was forged in the tumultuous context of 1930s Paris, where both artists sought refuge from societal constraints and nurtured their radical creativity within the vibrant literary circle of Montparnasse. Immersed in the avant-garde movement, they embraced existentialism, surrealism and radical individualism, striving to redefine the boundaries of literature and art. This bohemian ethos permeated their personal and creative relationship, underlining a mutual reverence for raw emotion, an uninhibited exploration of the human psyche and a fervent rejection of societal norms. With Nin's deep introspection and Miller's unabashed prose, their symbiotic influence on each other's work has unfolded an intellectual and emotional synergy that continues to captivate scholars and enthusiasts alike. The Bohemian bond also embodies a profound sense of liberation from societal conformity, as both Nin and Miller challenged the conventions of morality, gender roles and artistic expression in their daring quest for authentic living and creation. Their willingness to push boundaries not only challenged the status quo, but also redefined the very essence of literary and interpersonal relationships. As we delve into the twists and turns of this bohemian bond, we discover unbridled passion, relentless iconoclasm and an enduring alliance that transcended the boundaries of time and space, leaving an indelible mark on the literary landscape.

The relationship between Henry Miller and Anaïs Nin is characterised by a labyrinth of emotions, conflicts and reconciliations. The complexity of their friendship reflects the tumultuous nature of their personal lives and literary activities. At times, their relationship appeared to be a harmonious convergence of kindred spirits, each drawing inspiration from the other's creative energy. However, this idyllic façade was often shattered by intense disagreements and emotional turmoil. Their interactions were marked by a constant interplay of admiration, romance, jealousy and resentment, creating a dynamic that transcended the conventional boundaries of friendship. Despite these challenges, their bond withstood many trials, reflecting an enduring resilience and mutual understanding. It is a friendship that has thrived in adversity, always seeking reconciliation and renewal.

A wider circle: Allies and acquaintances in literature

Henry Miller's literary career was shaped not only by his complex friendship with Anaïs Nin, but also by a wider circle of allies and acquaintances in the world of literature. As a maverick in the literary landscape, Miller was inspired by and engaged with a wide range of writers, poets and thinkers who left an indelible mark on the evolution of his creation. A notable figure in this sphere was Lawrence Durrell, whose unconventional approach to narrative and exploration of existential themes resonated deeply with Miller. Their interactions gave rise to a rich exchange of ideas, influencing each other's work and contributing to the wider intellectual discourse of their time.

Miller's exchanges with eminent literary figures such as T.S. Eliot, Ezra Pound and William Carlos Williams further broadened his intellectual horizons, fostering an environment of robust intellectual exchange that propelled the development of his literary voice. In addition, Miller's immersion in the vibrant expatriate community of Paris brought him into contact with luminaries such as Gertrude Stein, whose avant-garde approach to literature and patronage of emerging talent provided fertile ground for artistic experimentation and collaboration. The bohemian enclave in which Miller found himself was brimming with creative energy, which enabled him to meet kindred spirits such as Djuna Barnes, who challenged conventional narrative forms and offered alternative perspectives on gender and identity.

These alliances and interactions not only enriched Miller's own literary activities, but also contributed to the rise of experimental and innovative writing in the wider literary landscape. In addition, the friendships and connections forged during Miller's travels, particularly in Greece and the Mediterranean region, introduced him to the works of Nikos Kazantzakis and Constantine P. Cavafy, among others, whose distinct voices and cultural influences left an indelible imprint on Miller's worldview and writing. By immersing himself in the diversity of literary circles, Henry Miller not only found kindred spirits and intellectual provocateurs, but also forged lasting bonds that reverberated throughout his work, offering a glimpse into the intertwined nature of artistic expression and the power of collective creativity.

Intellectual exchanges and their influence on the works

Intellectual exchange within literary circles was a dynamic force that profoundly influenced the works of Henry Miller and Anaïs Nin. Their interactions with others, such as D.H. Lawrence, e.e. cummings and Lawrence Durrell, provided a rich tapestry of ideas and perspectives that invigorated their creative spirits. The atmosphere of bohemian Paris and the expatriate community nurtured a constant dialogue of artistic and philosophical exploration, fostering an environment conducive to intellectual growth.

These exchanges were not simply casual conversations, but rather intense discussions that challenged traditional norms and delved into the depths of existentialism, surrealism and the human psyche. These dialogues stimulated the development of Miller's raw, unabashed prose, while inspiring Nin to cultivate her introspective, emotionally charged narratives. The fusion of their distinct voices with ideas gleaned from their literary peers led to a transformative evolution in their respective writing styles, giving their works a nuanced depth that continues to captivate readers to this day.

The impact of these intellectual exchanges transcended mere literary know-how; it permeated the thematic essence of their works, giving them a profound sense of interconnectedness, authenticity and rebellion against societal constraints. Themes such as sexual liberation, the quest for spiritual enlightenment and the celebration of individuality were interwoven into their stories, reflecting the passionate debates and revelations that took place within their literary circles.

Moreover, the influence of these exchanges extended beyond the pages of their own works, seeping into the wider cultural landscape. Their provocative ideas and fervent discourses contributed to the intellectual effervescence of the time, leaving an indelible mark on the trajectory of literature and paving the way for future generations of writers and thinkers. The intellectual exchange thus bears witness to Miller and Nin's enduring legacy, and highlights the transformative power of collaborative creativity and the profound impact of collective intellectual inquiry on the evolution of literature.

Public perception and private realities

Exploring the dichotomy between public perception and private realities in the lives of literary figures offers insight into the complex nature of their existence. While renowned authors often become larger-than-life personalities through their works, speeches and public personas, their private lives remain shrouded in secrecy, introspection and vulnerability. Anaïs Nin and her contemporaries were no exception to this phenomenon, as their public image was framed by the ideologies they presented in their literature, while their private lives navigated a web of emotions, desires and struggles.

Anaïs Nin, like many of her peers, carefully nurtured her public image to match her artistic philosophies and intellectual pursuits. Through her published works and public appearances, she projected an image of independence, sensuality and freedom of spirit that captivated readers and admirers alike. Behind the curtain of public recognition, however, her personal life is marked by deep inner conflicts, unconventional relationships and private writings that reveal the depth of her emotional landscape. Beyond Nin, many literary figures have faced a similar dissonance between their public persona and their private struggles, challenging the simplistic narratives constructed around their public identities. F. Scott Fitzgerald, Ernest Hemingway and Sylvia Plath are just a few examples of writers whose public legacies have belied the intricate tapestries of their private experiences.

The lure of fame and recognition has often cast a shadow over the multiple realities of these authors, perpetuating myths and misconceptions about their personal lives. As readers and researchers, it is essential to untangle the threads of public perception from the complex web of private realities, recognising that the true essence of these literary icons extended far beyond their public personas. By better understanding the private truths that shaped their lives and work, we gain a better understanding of the human condition, empathise with their struggles and better appreciate the complexities inherent in the marriage of art and life. Ultimately, this exploration prompts us to reassess our interactions with literature, inviting us to engage with the intimate vulnerabilities of authors and the transformative power of their private revelations.

Legacy in the evolution of literary movements

As we face the formidable task of assessing Henry Miller's legacy within the evolution of literary movements, it becomes clear that his impact is indelible and multifaceted. Miller's revolutionary works, characterised by their unbridled frankness and raw emotional intensity, have left a lasting imprint on the literary landscape. By challenging traditional narrative structures and unabashedly exploring taboo subjects, he challenged established conventions, marking a radical shift in the trajectory of literary expression.

At the heart of Miller's legacy is the profound influence he exerted on subsequent generations of writers. The subversive nature of his prose and his uncompromising commitment to authenticity inspired a pantheon of countercultural and avant-garde literary movements. From the Beat Generation to the psychedelic revolution of the 1960s, Miller's ethos permeated the zeitgeist, spawning a fervent reimagining of the artist's role in society.

Moreover, Miller's legacy extends beyond the boundaries of American literature, resonating around the world with writers seeking to break free from conventional literary constraints. His thematic preoccupations with existential angst, human sexuality and the tumultuous vicissitudes of life have provided a model for introspective and confessional writing, influencing a wide range of international literary movements, from the Latin American boom to European existentialism.

Moreover, Miller's unvarnished depiction of the human condition and his unabashed celebration of the sensual and visceral aspects of existence precipitated a paradigm shift in the perception of literature as an agent of social change. By dismantling entrenched taboos and exposing society's hypocrisies, Miller encouraged future generations of writers to harness the power of literature as a catalyst for introspection, critique and revolution.

Finally, Miller's legacy is intimately linked to the current discourse on censorship and artistic freedom. His long battles against censorship and his unwavering defence of freedom of expression have galvanised writers around the world, sparking crucial debates about the right of artists to interrogate human experience without constraint. Indeed, Miller's legal victories and unyielding advocacy of creative autonomy continue to reverberate in contemporary conversations about the limits of artistic license and the responsibilities of creators.

In conclusion, Henry Miller's enduring legacy in the evolution of literary movements transcends the boundaries of genre or era, embodying a relentless spirit of rebellion, authenticity and intellectual daring. His writings are a timeless testament to the transformative potential of literature and the enduring resonance of an artist unafraid to travel the uncharted paths of human experience.

14

A Philosopher of Everyday Life

The philosophy of everyday life

MUNDANE EXPERIENCES, OFTEN REGARDED as ordinary and insignificant, play a profound role in the formation of philosophical ideas. The tapestry of everyday life conceals a wealth of wisdom just waiting to be unravelled. It is in seemingly banal moments that the essence of human existence is revealed most vividly. Sipping a cup of coffee in the morning, watching the autumn leaves dance, or simply strolling down a busy city street are all open doors to introspection and contemplation. These ordinary events, when viewed through a philosophical lens, become imbued with transcendent meaning. They provide an opportunity for profound reflection on the human condition and the very nature of reality. At their core, mundane experiences remind us of our common humanity and the interconnectedness of all things.

By immersing ourselves in the philosophy of the mundane, we learn to better appreciate the subtle nuances of existence. Routine and commonplace become rich sources of existential interrogation, offering profound insights into the nature of being. By closely examining these everyday encounters, we discover layers of meaning and significance that might otherwise have eluded us. This process allows us to cultivate a sense of attention and presence, enabling us to engage fully with the world around us. We realise that philosophical wisdom is not confined to lofty abstractions or esoteric theories, but can be found in the very fabric of our daily lives. Adopting the philosophy of the mundane fosters a deeper connection with reality and a heightened awareness of the beauty and depth inherent in the most ordinary moments. Such an approach invites us to explore the deeper implications of the seemingly trivial, and encourages us to look for philosophical insight in the most unexpected places. Ultimately, it is by recognising the depth of the seemingly mundane that we are able to unlock a more enriched and meaningful mode of existence, allowing us to approach life with a renewed sense of wonder and appreciation.

Interpreting everyday experiences

Living in the everyday fabric of life, Henry Miller masterfully navigated the tapestry of existence, extracting profound meaning from seemingly mundane events. Through his lens, the ordinary becomes extraordinary and the mundane is transformed into a source of profound understanding. Miller's art lies in his ability to interpret the subtleties and nuances of everyday life, uncovering the mysteries hidden in the commonplace. His keen observations enable him to discern the poetry in routine and the beauty in banality, inviting readers to reconsider their own perception of the world around them. By delving into the microcosm of everyday experiences, Miller encourages us to appreciate the richness and complexity that underlie even the simplest moments.

In Interpreting Everyday Experiences, Miller invites the reader to accompany him on an intellectual journey through the familiar landscapes of everyday life. Through his evocative prose, he reveals how seemingly inconsequential events can take on profound symbolic meaning and reflect broader truths about the human condition. From the quiet reverie of a solitary stroll to the cacophony of urban streets, Miller deftly captures the essence of human experience, drawing universal themes from the tapestry of individual encounters. Each observation serves as a portal for introspection, prompting readers to assess their own lives with renewed clarity and depth. Interpreting everyday experiences becomes an exercise in mindfulness, an opportunity to elevate the mundane to the profound and to draw meaning from the seemingly trivial.

Moreover, Miller's exploration goes beyond mere observation, inviting readers to engage in active reflection and contemplation. The relentless search for meaning through everyday encounters compels us to approach life as a continual examination and interpretation of our surroundings, underlining the importance of cultivating a consciousness attuned to the pulse of existence. Through his art, Miller demonstrates that every fleeting anecdote or mundane event has the potential to produce limitless revelations when viewed through the lens of careful interpretation. In this way, he enables readers to extract wisdom from the fabric of their own lives, encouraging them to grasp the depth of the ordinary and engage with each moment as an opportunity for enlightenment.

The existential foundations: A practical approach

In exploring the existential foundations of everyday life, Henry Miller looks at the profound philosophical implications inherent in the everyday. His practical approach to existentialism involves a deep contemplation of the human condition in the context of ordinary experiences. Rather than engaging in abstract theorising, Miller encourages readers to adopt a practical philosophy rooted in the reality of everyday existence.

Central to Miller's exploration is the idea that human nature is profoundly shaped by the way in which individuals confront the challenges and triumphs of everyday life. He emphasises the importance of acknowledging the contradictions and complexities inherent in human existence while seeking authenticity and meaning. By adopting a pragmatic approach to existential questions, Miller seeks to offer insights that can be applied to lived experience, enabling individuals to grapple with the fundamental questions of existence in a more tangible and relatable way.

In addition, Miller's practical approach to existential foundations extends to his examination of the interaction between individual consciousness and the external world. He asks how human perception, interpretation and interaction with the surrounding environment help to shape the individual's sense of self and purpose. Through this lens, he presents an existential framework that advocates introspection and mindfulness as essential tools for navigating the complexities of modern life.

This practical approach also involves a nuanced appreciation of human interconnectedness and the wider fabric of society. Miller argues that authentic existential engagement requires an awareness of collective human experience and how individuals are interwoven into the communal tapestry of existence. By recognising the shared struggles and aspirations that characterise human nature, Miller advocates a compassionate and empathetic orientation towards others, positioning these interpersonal dynamics as central to the existential journey.

Ultimately, Miller's practical approach to existential foundations is a compelling invitation to engage with deep philosophical concepts in a grounded and accessible way. By weaving together the ordinary and the extraordinary, he demonstrates the transformative potential of an existential perspective firmly grounded in the everyday realities of human life.

Observations on human nature

Human nature, as seen by Henry Miller, is a complex interplay of contradictions and universalities that shape the human experience. Miller's astute observations delve deep into the psyche and behaviour of individuals, exposing the complex layers of the human condition. His insight reflects an unwavering fascination with the duality of human nature, which is capable of both profound compassion and unfathomable cruelty. This paradoxical nature, as portrayed by Miller, bears witness to the perpetual struggle and growth inherent in the human journey. Moreover, his observations echo the enduring themes of vulnerability, resilience and the unwavering search for meaning that define human existence.

One of the remarkable aspects of Miller's exploration of human nature is his raw and uncompromising depiction of the baser instincts and desires that drive human behaviour. He highlights the intrinsic elements of lust, jealousy and rage, acknowledging their presence without moral judgement, but rather as integral components of the human tapestry. In doing so, Miller offers a glimpse into the untamed aspects of the human psyche, forcing readers to confront their own inner complexities. Equally captivating are Miller's reflections on the search for connection and intimacy, and the inevitable conflicts that arise from the clash between individual aspirations and the collective norms of society. His acute understanding of the nuances of human relationships and social dynamics resonates deeply, illuminating the subtleties of love, friendship and the evolving dynamics of human interaction. Moreover, his observations elucidate the perpetual oscillation between loneliness and companionship, and the never-ending desire for understanding and acceptance in the fabric of human society. Through Miller's perceptive eyes, human nature emerges as a complex mosaic, shaped by a multitude of influences ranging from personal experiences to wider cultural and historical contexts. This holistic perspective invites us to contemplate the interconnectedness of individuals within the wider framework of humanity. These observations serve as poignant reminders of the inherent universality and uniqueness of each individual, transcending geographical, temporal and ideological boundaries. Ultimately, Miller's profound observations on human nature exalt the multifaceted essence of the human spirit, encapsulating both its fragility and its unshakeable fortitude, while evoking a profound sense of empathy and understanding for man's odyssey.

Moments of epiphany in everyday life

Life is often a whirlwind of mundane routines and ordinary experiences. However, hidden in the folds of everyday life is the potential for extraordinary realisations - moments of epiphany that illuminate everyday life with profound meaning. These moments of clarity can occur unexpectedly, triggered by seemingly innocuous events or encounters. It was in these fleeting moments that Henry Miller found inspiration and enlightenment. Through observation and introspection, Miller elevated the mundane to the extraordinary, revealing the beauty hidden in the rhythms of everyday life.

Basically, the concept of epiphany in everyday life revolves around heightened awareness and the ability to discern the extraordinary in the ordinary. For Miller, this has manifested itself in various forms: a chance encounter on a busy street corner, the luminous glow of a sunset or the moving melody of a busker. Each of these moments offers a glimpse into the interconnectedness of existence and the depth of human experience. In recounting these moments, Miller invites readers to embrace their own capacity for transcendence in the seemingly trivial aspects of life.

The essence of epiphany in everyday life lies in its power to imbue mundane events with layers of meaning and significance. By recognising these moments of clarity, individuals can navigate the complexities of life with renewed insight and purpose. In essence, the search for epiphany in everyday life becomes a transformative journey - a pilgrimage through the ordinary towards a greater understanding of oneself and the world at large.

What's more, these moments of realisation often serve as catalysts for personal growth and evolution. They encourage individuals to reflect on their beliefs, values and aspirations, prompting them to constantly discover and update themselves. By exposing these moments of transformation, Miller emphasises how everyday experiences can shape a person's worldview and foster a profound sense of belonging to the great mosaic of humanity.

Through her evocative stories and philosophical reflections, Miller encourages readers to actively seek out these moments of epiphany, urging them to cultivate a mindset receptive to the subtleties of everyday life. In doing so, individuals embark on a profound quest for self-realisation and an enriched appreciation of what is remarkable in what seems unremarkable. By embracing these epiphanies, individuals can transcend the boundaries of the mundane, embarking on a journey of constant wonder and introspection.

Reimagining the ordinary

In Reimagining the Ordinary, Henry Miller explores the notion of extraordinary beauty and meaning in the seemingly mundane aspects of everyday life. Through his masterful prose, Miller encourages readers to take a more contemplative and appreciative approach to their everyday experiences, urging them to look beyond the surface and embrace the profound richness hidden in the ordinary.

Miller's exploration of the reimagining of the ordinary is an invitation to transcend habit and routine. He challenges readers to take a fresh look at familiar objects, activities and events, encouraging them to become more aware of the world around them. In doing so, he argues that individuals can unleash a source of creativity, inspiration and enlightenment that lies latent in their immediate environment.

Drawing on his own experiences, Miller gives striking examples of how he has personally reimagined the ordinary throughout his life and travels. From the small details of urban landscapes to the subtle nuances of human interaction, Miller discovers beauty and depth where others would perceive only banality. Through his anecdotes, he illustrates the transformative power of looking at the world with unbridled curiosity and wonder.

Reimagining the Ordinary' is also a poignant reflection on the interconnectedness of all things. Miller emphasises the intrinsic value of every facet of existence, no matter how trivial it may seem. This holistic perspective fosters a greater sense of empathy, compassion and unity, all of which are essential to fostering harmonious coexistence with one's environment and fellow human beings.

Miller's approach to reimagining the ordinary resonates deeply with the teachings of Eastern philosophies, particularly Zen Buddhism and Taoism. The concept of mindfulness, so central to these traditions, aligns closely with Miller's philosophy, emphasising the importance of being fully present in each moment and embracing the beauty inherent in simplicity. By fostering an appreciation of the ordinary, individuals can cultivate a sense of tranquillity, equanimity and spiritual fulfilment, ultimately leading to a more rewarding and purposeful life.

In Reimagining the Ordinary, Henry Miller offers a profound and illuminating perspective on how to draw meaning, joy and wisdom from the seemingly mundane aspects of everyday life. His insights allow readers to embark on a transformative journey of self-discovery and existential enrichment, inspiring them to a deeper engagement with the world and a better understanding of what it means to truly live.

Influence of Eastern philosophies

Henry Miller's exploration of Eastern philosophies gave him a unique perspective on life, which profoundly influenced his literary works. Drawing on the wisdom of traditions such as Taoism, Zen Buddhism and Hinduism, Miller immersed himself in the teachings of simplicity, mindfulness and acceptance. These philosophies resonate with his desire to find meaning in everyday life, to discover the depth in the seemingly mundane. The Taoist concept of 'wu wei', with its emphasis on effortless action and natural spontaneity, found its way into Miller's approach to storytelling and life.

This principle guided his depiction of characters navigating the complexities of life with grace and without resistance, reflecting the Taoist ideal of harmonising with the flow of existence. Similarly, Zen Buddhism's emphasis on present moment awareness and direct experience has shaped Miller's prose, infusing it with an immediacy and authenticity that captures the essence of lived reality. His encounters with Hindu texts and practices have also left an indelible mark, leading him to contemplate the interconnectedness of all things and the cyclical nature of existence. In addition, the Eastern emphasis on detachment and non-attachment informed Miller's exploration of desire, suffering and liberation within human experience. By integrating these Eastern philosophical ideas into his writing, Miller invited readers to engage with his work on a deeper, more contemplative level. His prose became a vehicle for transmitting timeless wisdom, inviting readers to embark on inner journeys of introspection and self-discovery. Influenced by Eastern philosophies, Miller's work has transcended simple narrative, offering a profound commentary on the human condition and the quest for transcendence.

Transcendence through simplicity

By exploring the theme of 'transcendence through simplicity' in the context of Henry Miller's philosophical worldview, we understand the importance he placed on simplicity as a means of finding meaning and fulfilment in life. This notion of transcendence goes beyond mere material minimalism and penetrates deeply into the realm of spiritual and existential clarity. Miller celebrates the art of living authentically and in harmony with the natural rhythms of existence - a philosophy intrinsically rooted in the virtue of simplicity.

At the heart of Miller's perspective is the rejection of alien complexities and artificial constructs that stand in the way of authentic human experience. In his writings, he advocates a return to the essential elements of being, urging individuals to seek fulfilment in the unadorned and unvarnished aspects of life. The culture of simplicity is, for Miller, a path to inner peace and enlightenment, a way through which we can transcend the burdensome trappings of modernity and the expectations of society.

This transcendence moves away from conventional measures of success and encourages individuals to find solace in modest pleasures, everyday joys and the beauty of the mundane. Adopting a minimalist approach allows you to reframe your perception of the world and become aware of the interconnectedness of all things. In this way, simplicity becomes a means of experiencing moments of profound awe and wonder in the ordinary, from the delicate blossoming of a flower to the resounding laughter of a child. As such, simplicity serves as a transformative force, elevating the mundane to the extraordinary.

Moreover, Miller's advocacy of simplicity reflects an Eastern influence, aligning himself with philosophies such as Zen Buddhism and Taoism, which emphasise the tranquillity and wisdom to be found in simplicity. Echoing these traditions, Miller invites readers to contemplate the profound meaning of a decluttered life, free from the distractions that prevent true introspection and spiritual connection. Through the lens of 'transcendence through simplicity', Miller not only challenges society's dogmas, but also offers a guiding philosophy for those seeking a more meaningful and fulfilling existence. In doing so, he emphasises the value of simplicity as an instrument for transcending the constraints of contemporary life, revealing the depth and beauty of life's simplest moments.

The balance between despair and joy

Henry Miller's philosophical explorations in his literary works often delve into the dichotomous nature of human existence, addressing the delicate balance between despair and joy. By vividly and poignantly describing the tumultuous ups and downs of life, Miller provides a profound understanding of the human condition. By contemplating the existential struggles of his characters, he reflects on the universal experiences of suffering and fleeting moments of happiness.
The question is: how do we navigate this precarious balance?
Miller's elucidation of the interplay between despair and joy transcends mere intellectual enquiry; it becomes an emotional and spiritual journey for both the characters in his stories and the readers who accompany them. The depiction of despair is not simply a plunge into despair, but rather a recognition of the darkness that coexists with the light. It is a recognition of the depth of human suffering, an essential aspect of the human experience. Miller's characters confront this despair head-on, plumbing its depths to find meaning and endurance in life's trials. The presence of joy,

on the other hand, is depicted as a radiant force that pierces the gloom, illuminating even the most mundane moments. We celebrate life's little triumphs, the fleeting pleasures and unexpected encounters that punctuate an otherwise arduous journey. This juxtaposition serves to highlight the profound beauty of life's fleeting joys, underlining their importance in the face of despair.

Miller also emphasises the symbiotic relationship between these contrasting emotions. The search for balance is not about eradicating despair or desperately clinging to fleeting moments of joy, but rather embracing the full spectrum of human experience. It's about navigating the emotional terrain with resilience and grace, accepting the ebb and flow of life without succumbing to extremes. Moreover, Miller's philosophy goes beyond individual experiences to encompass a broader perspective of the human condition. His ideas incite introspection, encouraging readers to contemplate their own relationships with despair and joy. In doing so, Miller invites us to recognise the inevitability of hardship and to seek solace in the fleeting but profound moments of joy that punctuate our lives. Ultimately, Miller's exploration of the balance between despair and joy conveys a timeless lesson: by embracing the totality of our experiences, we discover the wisdom necessary to navigate the complexities of life with compassion, fortitude and grace.

A legacy of lived wisdom

Henry Miller's profound insights into human experience and his ability to navigate life's twists and turns continue to resonate with readers of all generations, cementing his enduring legacy as a philosopher of everyday life. This legacy encompasses the tangible wisdom drawn from Miller's lived experiences, as well as the intangible lessons woven through the living tapestry of his literary works. Miller's raw and unflinching portrayals of joy, despair, love and everyday life convey timeless truths that serve as a guide for those seeking authenticity in an increasingly complex world.

Miller's legacy goes beyond the simple recounting of personal anecdotes; it lies in the depths of his philosophy, where disillusionment meets hope, and chaos is accepted as part of the human condition. His lived wisdom offers comfort to those grappling with the contradictions inherent in existence, providing a roadmap for reconciling life's polarities. From seemingly mundane details to grand epiphanies, Miller encourages readers to seek meaning and purpose in every facet of their lives, fostering a deep appreciation of the beauty inherent in the ordinary.

The impact of Miller's lived wisdom transcends geographical and temporal boundaries, seeping into contemporary consciousness with undiminished relevance. His fervent commitment to extracting truth from the mundane serves as a beacon for individuals navigating the complexities of modernity, offering respite from the cacophony of superficiality that often dominates the cultural landscape. Moreover, Miller's legacy evokes a profound sense of introspection, compelling readers to reassess their own lives and relationships with new clarity and compassion.

In addition, Miller's lived wisdom continues a rich tradition of philosophical inquiry imbued with unwavering authenticity. She encourages us to move away from conventional modes of philosophical discourse by rooting ourselves in the visceral realities of life. By interweaving the personal with the universal, Miller passes on invaluable lessons about resilience, self-discovery and the pursuit of truth, ensuring that her legacy as a source of enlightenment and inspiration endures.

In essence, Henry Miller's enduring legacy as a philosopher of everyday life continues to enrich the literary and philosophical landscape with its profound resonance and enduring relevance. His lived wisdom, honed over a lifetime of introspection and experimental exploration, testifies to the enduring power of authentic expression and existential insight. As readers peruse the pages of Miller's works, they are not mere spectators, but participants in a collective odyssey, where the ordinary becomes extraordinary and the mundane reveals its extraordinary truth.

15

Controversy and Criticism

Reception Through the Decades

Introduction to controversy

Henry Miller's literary works have long been surrounded by controversy, provoking strong reactions from the public and literary critics alike. The nature of these controversies can be attributed to the provocative and uncompromising depiction of human desire, sexuality and existential themes in his writing. Miller's innovative approach to depicting the raw, unfiltered aspects of life challenges societal norms and tests the boundaries of artistic expression. His frank exploration of taboo subjects such as sexual liberation, individualism and anti-establishment sentiments immediately attracted attention and scrutiny from readers and authorities alike. As a result, his works caused shock and awe when they were first published, triggering discussions about censorship, morality and the limits of freedom of expression. The controversies surrounding Miller's writing have been fuelled by his uncompromising rejection of convention and his firm commitment to authenticity.

By fearlessly exposing the most intimate complexities of human existence, Miller confronted society's taboos and provoked visceral reactions from those who encountered his work. This confrontational approach to storytelling has often polarised audiences, dividing them into ardent supporters and vehement detractors. As a result, Miller's literature played a central role in challenging existing literary traditions and reshaping the cultural landscape of the time. The ensuing debates, legal battles and public discourses brought the issues of artistic freedom, censorship and moral responsibility to the forefront of public consciousness. Examining the origins of these controversies, it becomes clear that Miller's unyielding determination to peel back the veneer of societal convention and expose the raw, unadulterated realities of human experience provoked both fervent admiration and vehement condemnation. The lasting impact of these controversies continues to resonate, illuminating the complex interplay between art, society and individual expression, while consolidating Miller's status as a literary iconoclast.

Initial public reaction: shock and awe

The initial reception of Henry Miller's work in the 1940s and 1950s was characterised by a maelstrom of controversy, provoking both shock and awe among readers and critics. Viscerally raw and unequivocally frank, Miller's prose upended conventional literary sensibilities, challenging the societal and moral norms of the time. Tropic of Cancer, in particular, provoked vehement reactions because of its explicit content and its direct exploration of taboo subjects such as sexuality, nihilism and the human condition.

In the stifling atmosphere of post-war America, Miller's no-holds-barred depiction of the darkest aspects of life unleashed a storm of debate and condemnation. The graphic depiction of sexual relations and the unabashed examination of existential angst provoked a wave of moral indignation in conservative circles, triggering obscenity lawsuits and legal battles. As a result, Tropic of Cancer was banned in the United States for over twenty years, becoming a symbol of resistance to censorship and a focal point in the fight for freedom of expression.

Despite the fervour of the opposition, the novel also found fervent supporters who recognised the unparalleled honesty and intensity of Miller's writing. Intellectuals and artists rallied around Miller, seeing his work as a bold manifestation of artistic freedom and authenticity. This dichotomy of reactions underlines the profound impact and polarising nature of Miller's literary contributions, opening the way for an ongoing dialogue about the role of provocative art in society.

As shockwaves reverberated through literary circles, Miller firmly defended his artistic vision, rejecting the imposition of moral constraints and defending the artist's right to venture into controversial territory. His refusal to capitulate to societal pressures reinforced his perception as a literary iconoclast, increasingly revered for his daring break with conventional modes of storytelling.

Ultimately, the initial public reaction to Miller's work was emblematic of an era in the throes of unprecedented social and cultural upheaval, where traditional values clashed with emerging ideologies and expressions. The seismic impact of Miller's controversial literature transcended mere sensationalism, sparking an enduring discourse on the power, limits and responsibilities of art in confronting society's taboos and challenging dominant paradigms.

Critical reception in the 1940s and 1950s

In the 1940s and 1950s, Henry Miller's literary works received a tumultuous and polarising reception. His provocative and uncompromising exploration of human sexuality, societal taboos and existential philosophy challenged the norms of the time, provoking strong reactions from critics and audiences alike. The publication of Tropique du cancer in 1934 had already sparked controversy because of its explicit content and raw description of human experience. As a result, the 1940s and 1950s were marked by both fervent condemnation and passionate defence of Miller's writings. Critics at the time were deeply divided in their assessments, some dismissing his work as obscene and devoid of literary merit, while others praised it as a revolutionary revelation in personal expression and unbridled artistic freedom.

Miller's uncompromising approach to depicting the human condition sparked debates about the nature of literature, censorship and moral standards, shaping the cultural landscape of the time. The prevailing conservative attitudes and strict censorship rules of the 1950s, exemplified by the notorious Comstock laws and obscenity trials, resulted in Miller's works being suppressed and banned in various regions, placing him at the forefront of legal battles over the limits of free speech and artistic expression. In the midst of this tumult, a burgeoning countercultural movement began to view Miller as a symbol of rebellion and nonconformity, underscoring the evolving perception of his literary importance. It is in this unstable context that the critical reception of Henry Miller's work in the 1940s and 1950s reflects not only the contentious dynamics of literary evaluation, but also the wider socio-political conflicts that defined an era marked by moral conservatism and the emergence of radical social change.

Censorship battles and legal challenges

In the immediate aftermath of their publication, Henry Miller's works, including Tropic of Cancer and Tropic of Capricorn, were fiercely opposed by censorship boards and law enforcement authorities. The explicit language and graphic representations of sexuality were deemed obscene and led to lengthy legal battles. The publication of 'Tropic of Cancer' in the United States in particular faced numerous problems, including the confiscation of copies by the authorities and lawsuits. Miller himself experienced the intensity of these battles against censorship, as he faced obscenity charges that led to long and arduous legal proceedings. Despite the rancorous confrontations, Miller persevered in defending his literary freedom, seeing controversy as an essential component of his artistic expression.

The censorship battles extended beyond the United States to Europe and other regions where Miller's works gained notoriety. In the UK, 'Tropic of Cancer' was at the centre of an obscenity trial that influenced the country's approach to literary censorship. This legal dispute paved the way for a reassessment of the limits of artistic expression and the societal role of literature, ultimately challenging established norms and stimulating debate on freedom of expression and creation. In addition, the legal challenges surrounding Miller's writings triggered discussions about the cultural and moral dimensions of literature, questioning the intersection of art, morality and public decency.

In the midst of this tumultuous legal landscape, defenders of free speech and artistic freedom rallied around Miller, championing his cause and emphasising the intrinsic value of unfettered creative expression. Legal cases and appeals reverberated through the halls of academia, as scholars delved into the complexities of censorship, questioning established dogma and engaging in scholarly research in defence of artistic autonomy. This era of legal disputes and intellectual discourse catalysed a paradigm shift in the understanding of the relationship between literature and societal mores, fundamentally altering the narrative around censorship and artistic expression.

The enduring legacy of these censorship battles and legal confrontations continues to resonate in contemporary discussions of literary freedom and the responsibilities of creators and the public. Henry Miller's perseverance in the face of adversity illustrates the ongoing struggle for artistic autonomy, leaving an indelible mark on the evolution of literary censorship and the ongoing fight for freedom of expression.

The cultural change of the 1960s: A reappraisal

During the 1960s, Henry Miller's works were significantly re-evaluated in the context of a wider cultural shift. This transformative decade marked a period of unprecedented social change, rebellion against traditional norms and the emergence of a counterculture that sought to challenge established conventions. As the world grappled with the aftermath of the Second World War and the emergence of new ideologies and movements, Miller's provocative writings resonated with a generation that was challenging the status quo.

The rejection of censorship and the embrace of freedom of expression were key aspects of the cultural change of the 1960s. This new tolerance for controversial and subversive literature led to a re-evaluation of Miller's work, which had previously been subject to strict censorship and legal challenges. As boundaries were pushed back and taboos broken, Miller's candid and unabashed depiction of human experience resonated with those seeking authenticity and emotional truth in art.

In addition, the 1960s saw a growing interest in existentialism, psychoanalysis and Eastern philosophy, all of which had a profound impact on literary criticism and interpretation. Miller's exploration of existential themes and his uncompromising examination of the human condition placed his work at the forefront of these philosophical discussions. Scholars and researchers began to engage with Miller's work in greater depth, recognising the complexities and nuances contained in his writing. This reappraisal propelled Miller from the realm of the sensational to that of serious contemplation and critical analysis.

The socio-political upheavals of the 1960s also contributed to a re-evaluation of Miller's depiction of social structures and power dynamics. As the civil rights movement gained momentum and the feminist movement challenged entrenched gender roles, readers and critics re-examined Miller's treatment of sex, gender and race. The evolving discourse of equality and justice prompted a re-examination of her work, leading to important conversations about representation, privilege and the responsibilities of the artist.

Ultimately, the reappraisal of Henry Miller's work in the 1960s reflected a broader paradigm shift in cultural attitudes and intellectual inquiry. His writing, once considered scandalous and vulgar, underwent a profound metamorphosis, establishing itself as a touchstone for examining the intersection of literature, society and individual autonomy. The cultural shift of the 1960s provided fertile ground for the recontextualisation of Miller's legacy, giving his work a new relevance and complexity that continues to captivate readers and scholars alike.

Transcending scandal: academic perspectives

As the cultural landscape shifted in the wake of the 1960s, Henry Miller's controversial works began to transcend initial scandalous perceptions and attract the attention of academic circles. This shift in perspective led to a reassessment of Miller's literary merits, with the focus shifting from perceived obscenity to an exploration of his artistic and philosophical contributions. Scholars from a variety of disciplines have examined Miller's work, looking not only at the explicit content but also at the underlying themes of existentialism, individualism and the human experience.

A key aspect of the academic discussions surrounding Miller's work has been the recognition of his innovative narrative techniques and unique writing style. Scholars and literary critics have analysed Miller's use of stream-of-consciousness, autobiographical narrative and free prose, recognising his bold break with traditional literary conventions. This break, once seen as disruptive, has come to be recognised as pioneering and influential, contributing to the evolution of the novel as an art form.

Another crucial dimension explored by scholars is the global impact of Miller's writings beyond the confines of the mores of American society. Comparative studies have been undertaken to examine how Miller's works have resonated with international audiences and become part of cultural and literary movements around the world. The analysis highlighted the universality of Miller's themes and the way in which his writings capture the essence of the human condition, transcending geographical and cultural boundaries.

In addition, the scholars engaged in deep philosophical research inspired by Miller's works, delving into the existential and nihilistic undercurrents that permeate his novels. By rigorously examining Miller's depiction of the search for meaning in a chaotic world, scholars have probed the profound questions raised by his writing, contributing to existentialist discourse and deepening understanding of the complexities of the human psyche.

This academic reappraisal, motivated by a desire to move beyond controversy, has elevated discussion of Miller's work to a nuanced and scholarly level. Through extensive research, critical analysis and intellectual debate, Miller's place in the canon of modern literature has been carefully delineated, carving out a rightful place among the significant and lasting contributions to the literary world.

Global perspectives: reception beyond America

Henry Miller's literary works have elicited diverse and intriguing responses around the world, responses that reflect unique cultural differences and societal attitudes toward artistic expression. His provocative and uncompromising portrayal of human experience not only sparked debate and discussion within American intellectual circles, but also left an indelible mark on international literary communities. To fully understand the global reception of Miller's writings, it is essential to delve into the nuanced and multifaceted perspectives of different countries and regions around the world.

In Europe, and particularly in France, where Miller spent much of his life, his works received particular attention and became emblematic of an avant-garde literary movement. Despite initial censorship and hostility, Miller eventually found favour with French intellectuals and artists who admired his bold and uninhibited approach to narrative. His impact in Europe extended beyond France, resonating with readers and critics in England, Germany and other European countries, each reacting differently to the raw, visceral nature of his prose.

In Asia, Miller's influence took on a different hue, arousing both curiosity and criticism. While some Asian readers have been attracted by the existential themes and philosophical introspection present in his work, others have been apprehensive or resistant to the frankness with which he depicts human desires and conflicts. Reception in Asia thus reflects a complex interplay of cultural values and literary sensibilities, reflecting both admiration and scepticism towards Miller's unorthodox narratives.

From continent to continent, Miller's writings have permeated the hearts and minds of readers in Latin America, Africa and elsewhere, with translations sparking new conversations and interpretations in diverse linguistic and social contexts. Whether in the bustling metropolises of South America or the remote villages of Africa, the themes and characters woven into Miller's works have stimulated thought and discourse, underlining the universal nature of his stories.

In examining the global reception of Henry Miller's literary legacy, it becomes clear that his impact transcends national borders and cultural boundaries, leaving a rich tapestry of perspectives and ideas. The varied responses to his work reflect the enduring relevance and complexity of his writings, offering a compelling case study in the dialogue between literature and the many facets of human experience. By exploring the international resonance of Miller's work, we gain valuable insights into the interconnectedness of global literary cultures and the enduring power of narrative to provoke, inspire and unite.

Miller's place in modern literary criticism

Henry Miller's place in modern literary criticism is a subject of great complexity and enduring fascination. The provocative and unapologetic nature of his writing has provoked both adulation and disdain from literary scholars and critics around the world. At the heart of this debate is the question of Miller's contribution to the evolution of literature and the impact of his work on the cultural and intellectual landscape. In examining Miller's place in modern literary criticism, it is necessary to navigate a labyrinth of conflicting perspectives and discern the undercurrents that have shaped his reception.

It is impossible to ignore the fact that Miller's works, particularly 'Tropic of Cancer' and 'Tropic of Capricorn', provoked a seismic shift in traditional understandings of literary expression, pushing the boundaries of acceptability and challenging societal norms. This bold approach has made Miller a polarising figure in modern literary criticism. On the one hand, his supporters praise him for his unflinching honesty, revolutionary prose style and unyielding commitment to personal freedom. They argue that Miller's rejection of convention and his unabashed depiction of human experience have left an indelible mark on the literary world, inspiring countless aspiring writers to explore the uncharted territories of personal expression.

Conversely, his detractors claim that Miller's work is nothing more than shock value wrapped in a thin veneer of intellectualism, and that his disregard for conventional narrative structure and moral propriety renders his writings devoid of true artistic merit. However, despite these differences of opinion, it is undeniable that Miller's influence on modern literary criticism is perceptible in various forms, from the re-evaluation of obscenity laws to the re-examination of the limits of literary expression. By unabashedly embracing the raw and visceral, he forced critics to confront uncomfortable truths about the nature of art and its intersection with society. Moreover, Miller's challenge to literary conventions has forced scholars to re-evaluate the established criteria for assessing the artistic and philosophical depth of literary works, calling into question the very essence of what constitutes profound and powerful writing. In the maelstrom of conflicting opinions, Henry Miller symbolises the perpetual dialogue between tradition and innovation, morality and transgression, freedom and restraint in modern literary criticism.

Eminent critics and supporters : Discussion

Leading critics and supporters of Henry Miller's work have played an essential role in shaping the discourse around his literary contributions. Throughout history, Miller's writings have attracted both passionate defenders and vehement detractors, each significantly influencing the reception and interpretation of his work.

One of the most important discussions about Miller's work revolves around the themes he addresses and how they are perceived by different critics. On the one hand, Miller's supporters emphasise his unflinching portrayal of human desire, his fervent exploration of existentialism and his frank description of the human condition. They argue that Miller's raw, unfiltered style offers a poignant reflection on life, challenging conventional societal norms and inspiring introspection. These supporters often regard his works as daring and revolutionary, defending their literary merit and arguing for their inclusion in the canon of modern literature.

Conversely, critics have been quick to condemn Miller's writing as vulgar, obscene or morally repugnant. They argue that his graphic and explicit stories perpetuate obscenity and lack literary depth, dismissing them as mere shock value without substantial literary merit. In addition, some critics have criticised Miller's portrayal of women and minorities, citing examples of misogyny and racial insensitivity, adding layers of complexity to the debate.

The controversies surrounding Miller's works further intensify the discourse in academic circles, where scholars engage in in-depth debates about the author's artistic integrity and societal impact. Many contemporary literary theorists examine Miller's position in the context of literary history, considering how his works fit into the broader cultural and intellectual movements of his time. In addition, they explore the ethical implications of celebrating an author known for challenging societal norms and skirting the boundaries of acceptability.

A notable aspect of the discussion is the juxtaposition of Miller's influence on successive generations of writers. While some acclaimed writers ardently praise Miller's novels for their boldness and uncompromising vision, others express reservations about endorsing an author whose legacy remains mired in controversy and scandal. This disparity of viewpoints highlights the many facets of Miller's reception, evoking passionate exchanges on the moral, aesthetic and historical dimensions of his literary status.

Ultimately, the debate over Henry Miller's body of work transcends individual works and delves into fundamental questions about the intersection of art, morality and societal norms. It provides a rich tapestry for exploring the complex interactions between literature and culture, and offers a glimpse into the enduring power of the provocative and polarising voices that shape our understanding of humanity.

Conclusion: Enduring controversy, enduring impact

Over the decades, Henry Miller's work has remained a source of debate and fascination in the literary world. The enduring controversy surrounding the explicit content and unconventional narratives of his novels has ensured that Miller's impact continues to be felt long after their initial publication.

The lasting impact of Miller's writing lies in its ability to provoke critical thought and challenge societal norms. By challenging traditional literary conventions and tackling taboo subjects with unabashed honesty, Miller pushed the boundaries of what was considered acceptable in literature. His willingness to delve into the raw, often messy, aspects of human experience sparked profound discussions about art, censorship and the role of the artist in society.

Moreover, the controversies surrounding Miller's work have contributed to an ongoing reassessment of cultural and moral norms. Interpretations of Miller's writings evolve in tandem with societal attitudes. What was once considered scandalous and offensive is now re-examined from a more nuanced perspective, highlighting the transformative power of literature and its ability to challenge preconceptions.

It is important to recognise the diversity of reactions to Miller's work, ranging from fervent support to fierce criticism. This diversity of reaction underlines the complexity and richness of his literary legacy. While some continue to denounce his writing as morally reprehensible, others celebrate it as a bold and uncompromising depiction of the human condition. These different perspectives perpetuate the dialogue around Miller's work, ensuring that his influence endures and evolves with each generation.

In conclusion, the enduring controversy and impact of Henry Miller's work underlines its importance in the literary landscape. By provoking debate, challenging convention and redefining the boundaries of artistic expression, Miller's writings have left an indelible mark on the cultural and intellectual milieu. As we continue to grapple with the complexities of his legacy, one thing remains certain: Henry Miller's contribution to literature will continue to fuel discourse, inspire creativity and provoke thought for years to come.

16

The Personal Odyssey

A Search for Authenticity

The quest: Revealing the layers of the self

Henry Miller's introspective exploration of his multi-layered identity illustrates a relentless quest to transcend societal expectations and discover an authentic self. Delving into the crevices of his formative years, Miller uncovers the intricate tapestry of childhood roots and experiences that indelibly shaped his being. Through poignant memories and astute observations, he embarks on a profound odyssey to unravel the complexities inherent in his upbringing. The interplay of family dynamics, cultural influences and personal encounters becomes a canvas on which Miller paints a vivid portrait of self-discovery.

In recounting his early years, Miller is confronted with paradigm-shifting moments and formative experiences that left an indelible mark on his psyche. From the family home to the wider societal milieu, he meticulously analyses the influences and impressions that contributed to the construction of his identity. Unveiling the subtle nuances of interactions, conflicts and revelations, Miller offers readers a rich tapestry of memories that serve as the foundation for his quest for authenticity.

As Miller navigates the labyrinthine landscape of his past, he grapples with the imposition of societal norms and the constraints they place on individual expression. Confronted with the rigid structures that seek to shape and define him, he fervently seeks ways to transcend these conventional paradigms. In doing so, he highlights the complex interplay between societal constructs and the arduous path to self-realisation, challenging readers to question the veneer of societal conformity.

The quest to unveil the layers of self is a relentless pursuit, marked by introspection, retrospection and the reflections of a perceptive intellect. Miller's episodic recollections not only provide invaluable insight into his own journey, but also invite readers to embark on their own exploratory odyssey. Through his introspective prose, he urges individuals to sift through the layers of their own identity, provoking reflection and inciting contemplation on the multifaceted nature of human existence. By peeling back the layers of his past, Miller presents an allegorical narrative that resonates with universal truths and touches the heart of the human condition. Henry Miller's formative years were marked by a tumultuous childhood, which played an essential role in shaping his vision of the world and his literary sensibility. Born on 26 December 1891 in Yorkville, a German district of Manhattan, Miller was the first son of tailor Heinrich Miller and Louise Marie Neiting. His upbringing was characterised by financial difficulties and a turbulent family environment. These early experiences imbued him with a deep sense of introspection and resilience. Miller's childhood served as a crucible for his later explorations of human nature and society. The multiple challenges he encountered during those impressionable years left an indelible mark on his psyche, fostering both a rebellious spirit and a deep desire for authenticity. Despite adversity, Miller found solace in the rich tapestry of urban life, drawing inspiration from New York City's vibrant cultural milieu.

The city's diversity and dynamism would later seep into the fabric of his writing, infusing it with a raw, unbridled energy. Moreover, the multicultural tapestry of his childhood gave him an appreciation of the complexity of human existence, laying the foundations for his later explorations of identity and societal norms. By navigating the complex webs of poverty, family discord and social inequality, Miller developed an acute sensitivity to the nuances of human experience, an attribute that would come to define his literary work. This period of adversity and resilience laid the foundations for his unyielding commitment to unravelling the layers of human consciousness and societal constructs. Miller's early encounters with life's vicissitudes became the crucible from which emerged a relentless quest for truth and authenticity. In this way, his childhood roots and formative experiences serve as a crucial lens through which to understand the genesis of his unwavering quest for authentic expression and individuality.

Transcending conventional norms

Amidst the societal constraints and pervasive norms of his time, Henry Miller embarked on a remarkable journey of self-discovery and authenticity. Transcending conventional norms was not just an act of rebellion for Miller, but rather a profound philosophical and existential quest. Departing from the traditional path, he sought to challenge conventional wisdom and redefine the boundaries of literature and personal expression. At the heart of this transcendence is a fervent desire to break free from the shackles of society's expectations and embrace the raw, unfiltered essence of human experience.

Miller's radical break with conventional norms manifested itself in various facets of his life and work. His unyielding commitment to truth and authenticity permeated his literary works, as he fearlessly plunged into the complexities of human existence, unafraid to confront the uncomfortable truths often obscured by mainstream society. This insatiable thirst for authenticity led him to deconstruct established literary forms and to tap into the visceral depths of human emotion, challenging the very essence of what was considered acceptable or taboo in his day.

Miller's own lifestyle, moreover, testifies to his willingness to transcend conventional norms. Rejecting the trappings of materialism and society's expectations, he took refuge in simplicity and unbridled freedom. His nomadic wanderings, particularly in Paris and other European cities, not only provided fertile ground for creative inspiration, but also served as a crucible for intense personal transformation. In the midst of the decadence and disillusionment of the inter-war years, Miller's rejection of societal conventions stood out as a radical statement of individual sovereignty and unyielding determination.

Miller's unwavering stance against conformity and standardisation is reflected in his timeless words, echoing a call for all individuals to chart their own course and embrace the unvarnished truth of their existence. Her bold rejection of societal models and her relentless quest for authenticity continue to inspire generations of readers and creators to transcend the normative boundaries that limit their potential. Delving into Miller's quest for authenticity reveals the transformative power of embracing individuality and charting one's own odyssey through the stormy seas of societal expectations.

Paris: The catalyst for transformation

Amidst the cobbled streets and vibrant artistic milieu of Paris, Henry Miller found himself immersed in a transformative odyssey like no other. The City of Light, renowned for fostering creativity and innovation, became the crucible for a profound metamorphosis in Miller's identity. Wandering the boulevards and alleyways lined with bistros, he was captivated by the unshakeable energy that permeated every corner of the city. It was here that Miller met a wide range of thinkers, artists and revolutionaries whose unconventional lifestyles and avant-garde philosophies shattered his preconceived notions of existence.

In this bustling metropolis, Miller immersed himself in bohemian enclaves and salons where discussions ranged from the esoteric to the politically subversive. He met the likes of Anaïs Nin, who would become both his collaborator and his muse, and engaged in dialogues that challenged the very fabric of societal norms. Paris provided the fertile ground on which Miller's introspection flourished, fuelling a self-exploration that transcended geographical boundaries.

The city's artistic appeal extended beyond intellectual discourse into the realm of creative expression. In cafés and studios, Miller honed his craft, fervently transcribing the visceral essence of everyday life onto the pages of his manuscripts. The cacophony of the city, with its myriad voices and stories, served as a symphony that ignited in him a new clarity of purpose. Here, amidst the whispers of existential reflections and the echoes of cultural rebellion, Miller's voice acquired an unmistakable cadence, reflecting the untamed spirit of Paris itself.

Paris also gave Miller a heightened sensitivity to human experience, which manifested itself in a deep empathy that permeated his writing. The city's contrasts - opulence juxtaposed with squalor, tradition intermingled with avant-garde fervour - awakened in him a burning desire to delve into the raw emotions inherent in the human condition. This empathetic eye, honed and polished in the crucible of Paris, would become a defining characteristic of his literary legacy.

As Miller traverses the urban landscape, his personal philosophy evolves, shedding layers of societal conditioning and embracing a liberated authenticity. Amidst the bohemia and intellectual effervescence, Paris acted as the catalyst that ignited the dormant embers of his soul, propelling him towards a deeper understanding of himself. Ultimately, it was in the labyrinthine streets of Paris that Henry Miller's transformation from aspiring writer to unyielding literary iconoclast took root, leaving an indelible mark on his work and his vision of the world.

Introspection in Isolation: Diaries

Self-examination, linked to the limits of isolation, often finds its voice in the intimate practice of journaling and diary writing. Throughout his personal odyssey, Henry Miller sought solace and introspection in the written word, using diaries and journals as an unfiltered outlet for self-expression. In solitude and inner turmoil, he meticulously recorded his thoughts, emotions and experiences, unearthing profound ideas and revelations. Freed from the constraints of society, Miller's diary served as a canvas for raw, uncompromising introspection. Here, amidst the blank pages, is an unvarnished portrait of his most intimate struggles and triumphs.

In the sacred sanctuary of these journals, Miller embarked on a journey of self-discovery, navigating the labyrinth of his psyche with unwavering candour. Through writing, he fearlessly confronted his deepest fears, aspirations and insecurities, transcending the limits of conventional expression. These chronicles encapsulate the depths of his being, offering a cathartic release and serving as a testament to the complexity of human existence.

Moreover, the process of writing a diary gave Miller the autonomy to reflect on crucial moments and contemplate universal themes, unearthing profound philosophical reflections. By exploring the complexities of loneliness, love, longing and existential questions, his writings have become a testament to the power of introspection. They describe an individual's relentless quest for authenticity and illuminate the contours of the human condition with unparalleled depth.

By delving into himself, Miller has synthesised the chaos of his existential quest and transformed it into a repository of profound wisdom. These documents are a poignant testament to the transformative power of introspection and the transcendence of personal barriers. By immersing themselves in these deeply personal stories, readers bear witness to the unshakeable resilience of the human spirit and the enduring quest for self-realisation that defines our common humanity.

Navigating relationships and personal growth

As Henry Miller embarked on his personal odyssey in search of authenticity, exploring relationships and their impact on personal development became a crucial part of his journey. Navigating the intricate web of human relationships, Miller delved into the complexities of love, friendship and societal norms, unravelling the layers of his own emotional landscape. Through his interactions with a range of characters, both fictional and real, Miller has sought to distil the essence of human connection and its profound influence on the individual's quest for self-discovery.

In his reflections on relationships, Miller has grappled with the dynamics of intimacy and solitude, oscillating between the desire for deep connection and the yearning for solitary contemplation. His encounters with lovers, friends, mentors and adversaries provided fertile ground for introspection and self-examination, highlighting the complexities inherent in creating meaningful connections while preserving autonomy and authenticity.

Moreover, Miller's navigation of relationships served as a crucible for personal development, offering profound lessons in empathy, vulnerability and resilience. Against a backdrop of societal expectations and cultural mores, he confronted the dichotomies of closeness and distance, passion and disillusionment, idealism and pragmatism. These thematic tensions permeated his writing, infusing his literary works with a poignant depiction of the interplay between human bonds and the individual's existential journey.

Moreover, the subtleties of interpersonal dynamics underline the transformative power of relationships in shaping a person's perceptions, values and aspirations. Through the prism of her own experiences, Miller has probed the symbiotic nature of influence and reciprocity in relationships, tracing the ebb and flow of emotional currents that have influenced the evolution of her sense of self. Her nuanced portraits of characters and their interwoven narratives offer an incisive glimpse into the kaleidoscope of human interaction, encapsulating the universal quest for understanding, acceptance and belonging.

Ultimately, the process of navigating relationships and personal development became inseparable from Miller's quest for authenticity. Her introspective exploration of the human tapestry highlighted the profound interconnectedness of individual identity and community ties, reinforcing the eternal truth that our most defining moments often unfold in the crucible of relationships, testifying to the enduring resonance of the human experience.

Adversity as a means of self-discovery

Adversity is an intricate tapestry in the fabric of a person's life, weaving moments of challenge and struggle into a narrative of profound personal growth. Henry Miller's journey was punctuated by many adversities, each becoming a crucible for self-discovery. Through periods of financial destitution, artistic rejection and emotional turmoil, Miller's resilience and introspection transformed setbacks into transformative experiences. Adversity became her artistic muse, providing fertile ground for self-exploration and the excavation of inner truth. By confronting external obstacles and inner conflicts, Miller moved from mere survival to the pursuit of authenticity. His writings testify to the richness of the knowledge he acquired in the face of adversity. The tumultuous waters of hardship and misfortune often reveal the depths of a person's character. They force individuals to confront their fears, reassess their priorities and cultivate their resilience. Miller's encounters with adversity underscore the essential role it has played in fostering her unwavering commitment to self-expression and self-understanding. By exploring adversity, we discover the deeper meaning of these transformative experiences. They challenge our assumptions, broaden our perspectives and push us beyond our limits. Adversity becomes an indispensable catalyst, propelling us towards the discovery of our deepest capacities and potential. In Miller's case, adversity was not simply a series of unfortunate events, but a crucible where the dross of uncertainty and fear mixed with the gold of inner strength and courage. In the end, the journey through adversity revealed the latent reservoirs of creativity and resilience within him. The alchemical process of transmuting adversity into personal growth is a universal and timeless theme that resonates deeply with readers embarking on their own quest for self-discovery.

Philosophical foundations: The influence of existentialism

Existentialism, a philosophical movement that came to prominence in the twentieth century, had a significant influence on Henry Miller's personal odyssey towards authenticity. Rooted in the notion that individuals are responsible for creating meaning in their lives and must confront the absurdity and ambiguity inherent in existence, existentialist philosophy resonated deeply with Miller's exploration of self and reality. The fundamental principles of existentialism, notably individual freedom, choice and confrontation with the anxieties of human existence, are manifest in Miller's literary and personal journey.

Grappling with external constraints and internal conflicts, Miller drew inspiration from existentialist thinkers such as Jean-Paul Sartre, Albert Camus and Søren Kierkegaard, whose ideas he incorporated into his quest for authenticity. By adopting the existentialist approach, which emphasises lived experience and the rejection of dogmatic beliefs, Miller sought to dismantle societal norms and embrace the full spectrum of human emotion. His raw, unabashed description of life reflects the existentialist's insistence on facing up to the harsh realities of life without succumbing to despair.

In the culmination of Henry Miller's personal odyssey, the theme of authentic self-realisation emerges as a poignant and essential concept. Grounded in the existentialist philosophy that permeates his literary works, the journey towards self-fulfilment becomes a central focus. Throughout Miller's experiences, there is a gradual evolution from existential angst and introspection to a profound acceptance of the authentic self.

The influence of existentialist greats such as Kierkegaard, Nietzsche and Sartre resonates throughout this exploration, providing a rich tapestry of intellectual discourse and ideological contemplation. Ultimately, Miller achieves a profound understanding of himself, transcending societal constructs and embracing the authentic essence within. This culminating achievement testifies to the enduring relevance of Miller's personal odyssey in his quest for existential authenticity.

17

Conclusion

Embracing Chaos, Celebrating Existence

Reflecting on a journey: Synthesis of themes

In the rich tapestry of literature, Henry Miller's work embodies a tumultuous but deeply rewarding journey through themes that encapsulate the human experience. Through the amalgamation of chaos, sex, love and existentialism, Miller's writing transcends simple narrative and embraces a raw, unfiltered representation of the complexity of life. The synthesis of these major themes offers readers a profound insight into the visceral truth of existence. At the heart of Miller's exploration is the notion of embracing chaos as an essential component of creative expression. Here, chaos goes beyond mere disorder; it becomes a channel for artistic revelation, defying conventional norms and inviting a powerful and unabashed representation of reality. Within this chaos, Miller articulates the primal instincts and desires that underpin human relationships, presenting a raw and unvarnished examination of love, lust and desire.

This unvarnished honesty lays bare the tangled web of human emotions, providing a lens through which to explore the deepest complexities of human connection. Interwoven with these themes is the pervasive existential contemplation in which the characters grapple with fundamental questions of purpose, meaning and identity. Miller's synthesis of these existential explorations and the chaotic backdrop creates a thought-provoking picture that prompts readers to question the very essence of being. Moreover, the convergence of these themes is testament to Miller's unique philosophical perspective, which refutes society's expectations and confronts the contradictions inherent in the human experience. This synthesis invites readers to grapple with these contradictions, to revel in the messy and beautiful tangle of human existence. The power of Miller's synthesis lies in its ability to evoke introspection, to challenge preconceptions and to provoke a deep and resonant response in those who immerse themselves in his prose. It is in this synthesis that the beating heart of Miller's literary work lies - a compelling and fearless representation of humanity's raw and unyielding spirit in the face of chaos.

The role of chaos in creative expression

Chaos, often perceived as disruptive and destabilising, paradoxically plays an essential role in stimulating creative expression. In the chaotic whirlpool of life, Henry Miller skilfully navigated the tumultuous seas of emotion, experience and thought to extract the raw material for his literary endeavours. By embracing chaos not as an adversary but as a muse, Miller illuminated the complex relationship between disorder and creation.

In his magnum opus Tropic of Cancer, the chaotic, uncompromising narrative reflects the unpredictable fluctuations of life itself, forcing readers to confront their own existential disarray. Through this tumultuous portrait, Miller demonstrates that chaos is not only a destructive force, but rather a source of inspiration and innovation. By embracing the tempestuous nature of human existence, Miller has transcended conventional literary norms, fearlessly plunging into the messy depths of consciousness to unearth profound truths and universal ideas.

It is in this chaos that the seeds of creativity take root, springing up in uninhibited and unorthodox forms that challenge, provoke and, ultimately, enrich the human spirit. The incessant conflict and discord of life become the very catalysts of artistic ingenuity, driving the artist to exploit chaos as a powerful means of self-expression, introspection and societal critique. By recognising the intrinsic link between chaos and creativity, Miller invites readers to cultivate a deeper appreciation of the unpredictable cadence of existence, fostering an environment conducive to authentic artistic exploration. Whether in the frenzy of Parisian bohemia or the introspective solitude of his writing sanctuary, Miller revelled in the chaos of experience, extracting untamed emotions, unfiltered observations and unbridled passions to infuse his prose with unparalleled vitality and depth. In this way, chaos is not seen as an obstacle to be overcome, but as a crucible from which genuine creative genius emerges, akin to an alchemical transformation. As we immerse ourselves in the pages of Miller's work, we are confronted by the unsettling beauty of chaos, awed by the limitless possibilities it offers for self-discovery, growth and artistic transcendence.

Existential celebrations: A life well lived

Life, in all its chaotic splendour, presents us with a myriad of challenges and opportunities for self-discovery. Embracing the existential nature of our existence allows us to celebrate the very fact of being alive. Living well means navigating the paradoxes and contradictions that define the human experience. It's about finding purpose and meaning in the unpredictable flow of life. As Henry Miller demonstrated through his literary creations, a life well lived is one that dares to confront chaos with an unwavering spirit. It involves embracing the complexities of existence without succumbing to its uncertainties. The celebration lies not in the absence of restlessness, but in the resilience and fortitude displayed in the face of adversity. This joyful affirmation of life's inherent chaos and unpredictability is the mark of those who have truly lived.

In this celebration of existence, we encounter the interplay of joy and sadness, love and loss, success and failure. It is in these contrasts that the richness of life is revealed. Paradoxes abound, and it is in recognising and embracing these contradictions that a life well lived finds its depth. Authenticity emerges as a guiding principle, encouraging us to accept the dualities and incongruities that shape our paths. When we embrace the paradoxes of our own existence, we free ourselves from the pressures of conformity and pretentiousness. We discover the beauty of imperfection and the poetry of vulnerability. This is where the celebration blossoms, as we recognise that it is our flaws and contradictions that make us magnificent human beings.

At the heart of a life well lived is the cultivation of wisdom and insight. Through trials and triumphs, we accumulate knowledge and experiences that shape our understanding of the world and ourselves. Celebration comes not only from the accumulation of moments of joy and fulfilment, but also from the valuable lessons learned from moments of despair and desolation. It is the journey towards self-awareness and empathy that gives depth and meaning to our experiences. By searching for meaning and purpose in the midst of chaos, we unlock the potential for profound celebrations of existence.

Ultimately, a life well lived is marked by the imprint it leaves on others and on the world at large. Henry Miller's legacy bears witness to the lasting impact of a life fully engaged with the complexities of human existence. His works continue to provoke introspection and dialogue, inspiring readers to contemplate their own lives more deeply. By celebrating our own existence, we contribute to the collective tapestry of human experience, enriching the lives of those around us and leaving an indelible mark on the world. It is by celebrating life, with all its paradoxes and authenticity, that we draw out the true essence of our being and leave a lasting mark on the universe.

Paradox and authenticity: accepting contradictions

Accepting contradictions is the mark of a deeply examined life and, in Henry Miller's literary world, it is the very essence of authenticity. Through his work, Miller invites readers to confront the paradoxes inherent in human experience, recognising that the complexities of life cannot be categorised or rationalised. By confronting these paradoxes, Miller challenges conventional norms and invites deeper introspection about what it means to lead an authentic life.

At the heart of accepting contradictions is an understanding that life is intrinsically multiform. Miller's literature reflects the tension between order and chaos, love and disillusionment, hope and despair. It is through this exploration of contradictions that he captures the raw, unfiltered essence of existence, refusing to yield to its inherent disorder. In doing so, he conveys the message that true authenticity emerges by embracing the full spectrum of human emotions and experiences, unconditionally and without reservation.

Furthermore, embracing contradictions provides a deeper understanding of the human psyche. Miller's depiction of flawed characters and their complex relationships highlights the intricate interplay of conflicting emotions and desires. By delving into these contradictions, he paints a vivid portrait of the human condition, highlighting the struggle for self-discovery amidst the tumultuous nature of existence.

Moreover, the theme of paradox and authenticity resonates beyond the confines of Miller's literary universe. It is a poignant reminder that the profound truths of life are often found in the space between seemingly opposing forces. To accept contradictions is to accept the nuanced nature of reality, to recognise that certainty is rare and that authentic depth is found in the struggle with ambiguity and paradox.

In essence, by defending paradox and authenticity, Miller encourages readers to re-evaluate their own perception of the world. He urges them to look for beauty in chaos, to find meaning in contradiction and to strive for an authentic existence that transcends conventional constraints. Therefore, to truly embrace the fullness of life, one must confront its inherent paradoxes and celebrate the authenticity that emerges from traversing these complexities.

Literary giants: Influences and legacies

Literary Giants: Influences and Legacy: In delving into the fascinating world of Henry Miller, it is impossible to ignore the profound influences he has exerted on literary giants past and present. Miller's uncompromising approach to his craft and his willingness to tackle taboo subjects head-on have inspired a new wave of writers to challenge societal norms and embrace the raw, unfiltered essence of human experience. His literary legacy is far-reaching, stoking the flames of creativity for generations to come.

The unwavering impact of Tropic of Cancer, Tropic of Capricorn and other works not only shaped modern literature, but also cemented Miller's position as a revolutionary force in the literary landscape. From Jack Kerouac to Charles Bukowski, echoes of Miller's influence can be found in the works of countless authors who have dared to challenge conventional narrative. Throughout the annals of literary history, Miller's name stands as a testament to the enduring power of unfettered expression and unyielding individualism. His unabashed acceptance of human desires, flaws and complexities continues to serve as a guide for those seeking to chart their own literary course. While some consider his work shocking or controversial, there is no denying that Miller's fearless exploration of the human psyche has carved out an indelible place in the literary canon. His legacy lives on not only in the words he wrote, but also in the minds of readers and creators who find solace and inspiration in his daring spirit.

Indeed, Henry Miller is a literary titan whose influence transcends time, leaving an indelible mark on the literary zeitgeist. Through his unwavering commitment to authentic expression, Miller has left an eternal mark, ensuring that his towering influence will continue to shape and redefine the boundaries of literary art for generations to come.

An unyielding spirit: The affirmation of individualism

In the tumultuous landscape of literary history, Henry Miller stands out as a figure who embodies the inflexible spirit and affirms the philosophy of individualism with unshakeable conviction. Throughout his work, Miller fearlessly challenged societal norms and conventional thinking, defending freedom of expression and the search for personal truth. His unyielding spirit manifests itself in his refusal to conform to established literary conventions, choosing instead to chart his own course in the literary world. By embracing the raw, unfiltered nature of human existence, Miller boldly asserts the primacy of individual experience and the inherent value of personal expression.

At the heart of Miller's advocacy of individualism is a rejection of conformity and a commitment to authenticity. He celebrates the complexity of human emotions and experiences, refusing to sanitise or sugarcoat the often messy and chaotic realities of life. In doing so, he encourages readers to embrace their own singularity and cultivate an authentic connection with their deepest selves. Through his literary works, Miller encourages individuals to question prevailing orthodoxies and chart their own course, unhindered by societal expectations or external pressures.

Moreover, Miller's unshakeable belief in the power of the individual is underlined by his relentless pursuit of artistic freedom. He firmly defends the right of creators to explore the full spectrum of human experience without censorship or constraint. His uncompromising stance on creative freedom is a call to artists to fearlessly express their singular visions, unbound by external influences or limitations. Moreover, Miller's unwavering commitment to authenticity and individualism has resonated deeply with readers, generating a collective desire for authentic expression and personal liberation.

Miller's emphasis on the affirmation of individualism transcends the realm of literature, permeating various facets of human existence. His unyielding spirit is an enduring testament to the transformative power of individual action, inspiring countless people to break free from conformity and embrace the richness of their unique narratives. Through his indomitable ethos, Miller implores us to navigate our lives with courage and resilience, fully embracing the complexities and contradictions that define our individual journeys. In this way, Henry Miller stands as a shining beacon of unyielding spirit, guiding generations towards the noble quest of self-discovery and unwavering individualism.

A philosophical conclusion: the essence of being

Philosophy, in its unwavering quest for understanding and enlightenment, often comes to a dead end when it attempts to unravel the enigma of human existence. At the heart of this quest is the perpetual contemplation of the essence of being - a formidable philosophical quest that has titillated the minds of thinkers, poets and sages for millennia. In the tapestry of existence, the threads of individualism weave a complex narrative, interwoven with the shared experiences of humanity. In the midst of this complex tapestry, the concept of self becomes both a personal odyssey and a collective endeavour.

At the heart of this exploration is the notion of authenticity, a resolute commitment to embodying one's true essence in the face of societal pressures and existential uncertainties. The essence of being transcends the superficial trappings of material existence, plunging into the depths of consciousness and self-knowledge. It invites individuals to embark on an inner journey, navigating the labyrinthine corridors of the mind to unearth the immutable truths that resonate deep within themselves.

In the context of the literary landscape, many writers have grappled with the profound philosophical implications of existence, channelling their introspective reflections into timeless works of art. Their stories serve as mirrors reflecting the many facets of human consciousness, inviting readers to participate in a vicarious exploration of the human condition. Through their writing, these literary luminaries offer a glimpse into the existential vicissitudes that shape our perceptions, values and aspirations.

Moreover, the essence of being reverberates through the annals of history, imbuing the collective consciousness with enduring questions that transcend temporal boundaries. From Aristotle's contemplations on the nature of the soul to Sartre's existential interrogations, philosophical discourse on the essence of being continues to fuel intellectual discourse and contemplative introspection. It engenders a sense of interconnectedness and shared introspection, underlining the universal aspiration to discover profound truths about the human experience.

Ultimately, the search for the essence of being embodies a perpetual quest for meaning, purpose and enlightenment. It precipitates the convergence of individualism and universality, reconciling the subjective narratives of countless lives with the global tapestry of human existence. As we navigate the labyrinthine corridors of existence, the essence of being invites us to seek understanding, embrace authenticity and celebrate the intrinsic value of our presence in this great cosmic tapestry.

Engaging with the human experience

In his exploration of the human experience, Henry Miller delves deep into the complexities of existence, tackling the fundamental questions that have plagued humanity since time immemorial. Through his raw, emotional prose, Henry Miller invites readers to confront their own vulnerabilities, fears and desires, creating an immersive journey into the depths of the human psyche. Without fear, he peels back the layers of societal convention and exposes the raw, unfiltered essence of human nature, forcing readers to engage with the deep subtleties of their own experiences. Miller's masterful storytelling transcends simple narrative; it becomes a mirror reflecting the many facets of the human condition.

At the heart of Miller's examination is an unwavering commitment to authenticity and truth. His unflinching depiction of human emotions, desires and struggles resonates deeply with readers, provoking a profound catharsis that often defies conventional literary boundaries. By exposing the raw vulnerabilities and multiple dimensions of the human experience, Miller conveys a revelatory understanding of the interconnectedness of individuals.

Moreover, Miller's exploration transcends the individual, encompassing wider societal and cultural contexts. He contemplates the juxtaposition of joy and suffering, love and loss, provoking introspection and contemplation of the universal human experiences that bind humanity together. It is through this heartfelt engagement with the human experience that Miller compassionately invites readers to recognise the shared struggles and triumphs that define our existence, fostering empathy and understanding across diverse perspectives.

What emerges from Miller's poignant stories is a profound sense of interconnectedness and shared humanity, underscoring the beauty inherent in life's struggles and triumphs. Her fiery depiction of the triumph of the human spirit in the face of adversity invites readers to explore the resilience and tenacity that define the human experience, serving as a beacon of hope and solidarity amid the turbulent tides of life. Through her honest and compelling prose, Miller engages readers in an empathetic dialogue, encouraging them to engage wholeheartedly with the vast spectrum of human emotion and experience.

By immersing ourselves in the rich tapestry of Miller's reflections, we are compelled to recognise and accept the complex nuances of human experience. Miller's unparalleled ability to capture the raw essence of existence offers readers the opportunity for deep personal reflection and empathetic resonance, bridging the gap between author and audience. Ultimately, his work is a lasting testament to the power of literature to elicit empathy, provoke introspection and inspire meaningful connections that transcend temporal and spatial boundaries.

His legacy and impact on modern literature

Henry Miller's indelible legacy continues to reverberate through modern literature, offering writers and readers alike a glimpse into the complex intricacies of the human condition. His unvarnished, unfiltered style of storytelling has inspired countless authors to break the constraints of conventional narrative, forcing them to delve deeper into the often unexplored realms of emotion, passion and carnal desire. Miller's unyielding commitment to authenticity has laid the foundations for a literary landscape that dares to embrace truth in all its rugged glory, unravelling the many facets of human existence with unparalleled fervour.

The impact of Miller's work extends far beyond the realm of conventional literature, permeating various genres and media, redefining the very essence of personal expression. His unbridled exploration of the depths of human experience is a lasting testament to the inexhaustible source of creativity that continues to inspire contemporary writers the world over. From the visceral poetry of Bukowski to the uninhibited prose of Kerouac, Miller's idiosyncratic influence remains omnipresent, electrifying the pages of modern literature with a pulse of unwavering vitality.

Moreover, Miller's fearless confrontation with society's taboos and his unwavering advocacy of unbridled artistic expression have catalysed a paradigm shift in the way contemporary writers engage with their craft. By intricately weaving threads of unfiltered truth and absolute passion into the fabric of their stories, the authors pay homage to Miller's revolutionary spirit, perpetuating an ethos of boundless creativity and undisguised honesty. Moreover, the documentation of his personal odysseys and his relentless quest for self-realisation have emboldened a new wave of writers to delve into the depths of their own psyches, transcending the mundane and banal and venturing into the uncharted territories of introspection and revelation.

In essence, Henry Miller's coterie of literary masterpieces is an enduring testament to the transformative power of pure art. As modern literature continues to evolve, it does so under the irrefutable influence of Miller's bold storytelling, etching his indomitable legacy into the annals of literary history, ensuring that his profound impact will continue to resonate for generations to come.

Final thoughts: A celebrated life

As we come to the final reflections of this literary odyssey, it becomes clear that Henry Miller's impact on modern literature extends far beyond his immediate contemporaries. His bold rejection of societal norms and his relentless quest for an authentic existence resonate with writers and readers of every generation. Miller's unabashed celebration of life's chaos and contradictions is a call to embrace the full spectrum of human experience.

In contemplating Miller's celebrated existence, one is compelled to dwell on the profound implications of his rugged individualism. Through his provocative prose and unflinching wit, Miller invites us to confront our own fears and insecurities, urging us to forge our own paths with courage and conviction. His legacy goes beyond mere literary influence; he embodies an enduring philosophy, one that advocates the pursuit of truth, freedom and unbridled creativity.

Moreover, in examining Miller's impact on modern literature, it is impossible to ignore the way in which he profoundly challenged the conventions of narrative and narrative structure. By breaking down traditional boundaries and imbuing his work with raw, unfiltered emotion, Miller set a precedent for future writers to explore the complexities of the human condition without restraint. This unbridled experimentation continues to inspire contemporary writers to push the boundaries of creativity and authenticity.

Moreover, Miller's celebration of existence resonates not only in the realm of literature, but also in the wider tapestry of cultural and philosophical discourse. Her fearless exploration of pleasure, pain, love and loss embodies the universal human experience, inviting readers to engage with the depths of their own lives. Through his words, Miller implores us to confront the existential questions that permeate our consciousness and to discover our own truths in the chaotic symphony of existence.

As we bid farewell to this intellectual journey, it is abundantly clear that Henry Miller's celebrated existence serves as both a guide and a mirror reflecting the multifaceted nature of humanity. By embracing the complexity of our existence, exalting the paradoxes that define us and defending the indomitable spirit of individualism, Miller invites us to take part in the greatness of life with unwavering fervour and unyielding passion. His writing is a poignant reminder of the beauty and intrinsic value of every moment we live, urging us to celebrate our own lives with the same relentless ardour.

Selective Bibliography

Works

Novels

1. *Tropic of Cancer* (1934)

2. *Black Spring* (1936)

3. *Tropic of Capricorn* (1939)

4. *Sexus* (1949) – Part 1 of the Rosy Crucifixion Trilogy

5. *Plexus* (1953) – Part 2 of the Rosy Crucifixion Trilogy

6. *Nexus* (1959) – Part 3 of the Rosy Crucifixion Trilogy

Travel Books

7. *The Colossus of Maroussi* (1941) – A travelogue of Greece

8. *Big Sur and the Oranges of Hieronymus Bosch* (1957) – Reflections on life in Big Sur, California

Essays

9. *The Books in My Life* (1969) – An autobiographical account of the books that influenced him

10. *Remember to Remember* (1947) – Essays and reflections on art, literature, and philosophy

11. *Stand Still Like the Hummingbird* (1962) – A collection of essays

12. *The Air-Conditioned Nightmare* (1945) – Critique of American consumer culture

13. *Quiet Days in Clichy* (1956) – Short memoir about his time in Paris

14. *Sunday After the War* (1944) – A novella and essays reflecting on World War II

15. *Cosmological Eye* (1939) – Early essays and sketches

16. *To Paint Is to Love Again: Selected Letters of Henry Miller, 1930–1980* (1985) – Posthumous collection of letters

Short stories and anthologies

17. *Stories of China and Japan* (1947) – Short stories inspired by his

travels

18. *The World of Sex* (1940) – Collection of short stories and essays

19. *The Wisdom of the Heart* (1941) – Anthology of essays and short pieces

Poems

20. *Maximus and Other Poems* (1944) – Collection of poems

21. *Murder the Murderer* (1938) – Experimental poetry

Posthumous works

22. *Henry Miller on Writing* (1964) – Insights into his creative process

23. *Henry Miller's Reading List* (1987) – Compilation of books he recommended

24. *Reflections on Writing* (1992) – Posthumous collection of essays on writing

25. *Henry Miller: The Paintings and Drawings* (1992) – Artwork and commentary

26. *The Time of the Assassins* (1952) – Posthumously reissued essays and reflections

27. *The Intimate Notebooks: 1940–1952* (1998) – Personal diaries and musings

Other notable works

28. *The Cosmological Eye: Selected Writings* (1939) – Early essays and sketches

29. *An Open Letter to Ernest Hemingway* (1937) – Critique of Hemingway's work

30. *Moloch, or This Gentile World* (1971) – Novel exploring Jewish identity and anti-Semitism

Unfinished or partially published work

31. *The Tropics of New York* (unfinished) – Autobiographical novel set in New York City

32. *The Paris Years* (various fragments) – Unpublished manuscripts from his time in Paris

Books on Miller or referring to him

Alvarez, A. (1970). *The savage god: A study of suicide*. Harper & Row.

Anderson, M. (2006). *Henry Miller and American writing*. Continuum.

Baruch, S. (1984). *Henry Miller: The man and his world*. Associated University Presses.

Berman, J. (2008). *All that is solid melts into air: The adventure of modernity*. Verso Books.

Blodgett, H. E. (1995). *Henry Miller: The Tropics of Desire*. Twayne Publishers.

Boyd, H. (1992). *Henry Miller: Vision and revision*. University of Alabama Press.

Carrington, L. (1990). *Henry Miller: The painter as writer*. Southern Illinois University Press.

Charters, A. (Ed.). (1982). *The portable Henry Miller*. Viking Press.

Cohen, J. M. (1975). *Henry Miller: A writer's progress*. Thames and Hudson.

Crowther, B. (1976). *Henry Miller: The heat of vision*. Indiana University Press.

Davis, J. R. (1991). *Henry Miller: A critical study*. Macmillan.

De Grazia, E. (1992). *Girls lean back everywhere: The law of obscenity and the assault on genius*. Random House.

Dijkstra, B. (1995). *Idols of perversity: Fantasies of feminine evil in fin-de-siècle culture*. Oxford University Press.

Ellman, R. (1973). *The myth of Sueños: Henry Miller's Tropic of Cancer*. Yale University Press.

Fitch, N. (1989). *Henry Miller: A literary legacy*. State University of New York Press.

Gallagher, C. (2000). *Reading Henry Miller: A journey through the novels*. McFarland.

Goldstein, A. (1982). *The sacred in the profane: Henry Miller's fiction*. Peter Lang.

Gray, R. (1990). *Henry Miller: Beyond the limits*. Faber and Faber.

Hart, J. D. (1972). *The world of Henry Miller*. William Morrow.

Hassan, I. (1987). *The dismantling of the aesthetic tradition: From modernism to post-modernism*. Rutgers University Press.

Hollander, J. (1997). *The figure of echo: A mode of resemblance in poetry*. University of California Press.

Jacobs, L. (1984). *Henry Miller: The journey back*. Southern Illinois University Press.

Kaplan, M. (1991). *Henry Miller and the politics of desire*. University of Massachusetts Press.

Kennedy, J. G. (1985). *Henry Miller: The emergence of a modern consciousness*. Stanford University Press.

Kostelanetz, R. (1992). *Conversations with Henry Miller*. Limelight Editions.

Lewis, R. W. B. (1960). *The romantic predicament: A study of the literary sensibility from Wordsworth to Yeats*. Harper & Row.

Martin, J. (1983). *Henry Miller: The visionary outlaw*. St. Martin's Press.

Meltzer, D. (1993). *Henry Miller and the imagination of abundance*. North Atlantic Books.

Nicosia, G. (1997). *Exiled in paradise: Henry Miller abroad*. Paragon House.

O'Connor, F. (1966). *Henry Miller: The mind and the flesh*. Doubleday.

Rasmussen, D. (2000). *Henry Miller and the critique of civilization*. Cambridge University Press.

Sontag, S. (1966). *Against interpretation and other essays*. Farrar, Straus and Giroux.

Articles, chapters et other references

1. Astvatsaturov, A., & Voytsekhovskaya, O. (2018). Russian Rhizome of American Modernism: Concerning the Problem of Henry Miller's Anarchism. 4, 163–183. https://doi.org/10.22455/2541-7894-2018-4-163-183

2. Bean, W. B. (1961). The Henry Miller Reader. JAMA Internal Medicine, 108(6), 965–966. https://doi.org/10.1001/ARCHINTE.1961.03620120149029

3. Bochner, J. (2003). An American Writer Born in Paris: Blaise Cendrars Reads Henry Miller Reading Blaise Cendrars. Nineteenth-Century Literature, 49(1), 103–122. https://doi.org/10.1215/0041462X-2003-2006

4. Cowe, J. (2020). Killing the Buddha: Henry Miller's Long Journey to Satori. https://theses.gla.ac.uk/7105/

5. Dearborn, M. V. (1991). The Happiest Man Alive: A Biography of Henry Miller. https://www.amazon.com/Happiest-Man-Alive-Biography-Miller/dp/0671677047

6. Ernst, G. (2010). The Paris Years (pp. 243–270). Springer, Dordrecht.

https://doi.org/10.1007/978-90-481-3126-6_12

7. Ferguson, R. (2012). Henry Miller : A Life. http://ci.nii.ac.jp/ncid/BA27207160

8. Foster, S. (1964). A Critical Appraisal of Henry Miller's Tropic of Cancer. Nineteenth-Century Literature, 9(4), 196. https://doi.org/10.2307/440495

9. Gifford, J. (2008). Reading Miller's "Numinous Cock": Heterosexist Presumption and Queerings of the Censored Text. English Studies in Canada, 34, 49–70. https://doi.org/10.1353/ESC.0.0129

10. Glicksberg, C. I. (1971). Henry Miller: Prophet of the Sexual Revolution (pp. 123–142). Springer, Dordrecht. https://doi.org/10.1007/978-94-010-3236-0_10

11. Herian, R. (2014). 'How Long Do You Intend to Stay?': Desire Meets Proscription in the Subject in Henry Miller's Via Dieppe–Newhaven. The Liverpool Law Review, 35(1), 65–81. https://doi.org/10.1007/S10991-013-9145-9

12. Hoyle, A. (2014). The Unknown Henry Miller: A Seeker in Big Sur. https://www.amazon.com/Henry-Miller-Seeker-Big-Sur/dp/1611458994

13. Jackson, P. R. (1971). Henry Miller, Emerson, and the Divided Self. American Literature, 43(2), 231. https://doi.org/10.2307/2924239

14. Jensen, F. (2019). Miller and the Modern City (pp. 17–27). Palgrave Macmillan, Cham. https://doi.org/10.1007/978-3-030-33165-8_2

15. Jong, E. (1993). The devil at large: Erica Jong on Henry Miller.

16. Masuga, K. (2010). Henry Miller and the Book of Life. Texas Studies in Literature and Language, 52(2), 181–202. https://doi.org/10.1353/TSL.0.0050

17. Masuga, K. (2011). Henry Miller and How He Got That Way. http://ci.nii.ac.jp/ncid/BB0926599X

18. Masuga, K. (2011). The Secret Violence of Henry Miller. https://www.amazon.com/Violence-Studies-American-Literature-Culture/dp/1571134840

19. Michel, G. (2018). "Beautiful and good things": The Dress of Anaïs Nin, 1931-1932. https://lib.dr.iastate.edu/etd/17268/

20. Nabholz, A.-C. (2004). The crisis of modernity: culture, nature, and the modernist yearning for authenticity. https://doi.org/10.5451/UNIB

AS-004290694

21. Nesbit, T. (2007). Henry Miller and religion. https://www.amazon.com/Miller-Religion-Studies-Literary-Authors/dp/041595603X

22. Parkin, J. (1991). Henry Miller: The Modern Rabelais. http://ci.nii.ac.jp/ncid/BA74592872

23. Sarangi, I. (2012). Miller and Women. IOSR Journal of Humanities and Social Science, 4(5), 9–12. https://doi.org/10.9790/0837-0450912

24. Skovajsa, O. (2014). Psaný hlas: Whitmanovy Listy trávy (1855) a Millerův Obratník Raka.

25. Sotiropoulos, L. (2017). Henry Miller Travels in Greece. Journeys, 18(2), 65–81. https://doi.org/10.3167/JYS.2017.180204

26. Stevenson, G. (2020). Henry Miller and the Beats: An Anti-humanist Precedent (pp. 19–57). Palgrave Macmillan, Cham. https://doi.org/10.1007/978-3-030-47760-8_2

27. Turner, F. W. (2012). Renegade: Henry Miller and the Making of "Tropic of Cancer." https://www.amazon.com/Renegade-Miller-Making-Tropic-America/dp/0300149492

28. Zhang, Y. (2023). National self-identification of the emigrant hero in the emigrant prose of Georgy Ivanov and Henry Miller. Article One: Loss of primordial national world and love. Tekst, Kniga, Knigoizdanie, 31, 6–24. https://doi.org/10.17223/23062061/31/2

www.ingramcontent.com/pod-product-compliance
Lightning Source LLC
Chambersburg PA
CBHW021402290426
44108CB00010B/355